Leading School Change

Nine Strategies to Bring *Everybody* on Board

Todd Whitaker

EYE ON EDUCATION
6 DEPOT WAY WEST, SUITE 106
LARCHMONT, NY 10538
(914) 833-0551
(914) 833-0761 fax
www.eyeoneducation.com

For information about permission to reproduce selections from this book, write: Eye On Education, Permissions Dept., Suite 106, 6 Depot Way West, Larchmont, NY 10538

Library of Congress Cataloging-in-Publication Data

Whitaker, Todd, 1959-
Leading school change: 9 strategies to bring everybody on board / Todd Whitaker.
  p. cm.
  Nine strategies to bring everybody on board
 ISBN 978-1-59667-131-7
1. School improvement programs. 2. Educational change. 3. Educational innovations. 4. Educational leadership. I. Title.
  LB2822.8.W55 2009
  371.2'07--dc22

                                                        2009030318

10 9 8 7 6 5 4 3 2 1

Other Titles by Todd Whitaker

What Great Teachers Do *Differently*:
Fourteen Things that Matter Most
Todd Whitaker

What Great Principals Do *Differently*:
Fifteen Things that Matter Most
Todd Whitaker

50 Ways to Improve Student Behavior:
Simple Solutions to Complex Challenges
Annette Breaux and Todd Whitaker

Dealing with Difficult Teachers, 2/E
Todd Whitaker

Seven Simple Secrets:
What the Best Teachers Know and Do!
Annette Breaux and Todd Whitaker

Dealing with Difficult Parents
(and Parents in Difficult Situations)
Todd Whitaker and Douglas J. Fiore

Motivating and Inspiring Teachers:
The Educator's Guide for Building Staff Morale
Todd Whitaker, Beth Whitaker, Dale Lumpa

Teaching Matters
Motivating and Inspiring Yourself
Todd and Beth Whitaker

Dedication

I would like to dedicate this book to my wife Beth. She has led me to change (mostly for the better) more than I ever thought possible. I love you.

About the Author

Dr. Todd Whitaker has been fortunate to be able to blend his passion with his career. He is recognized as a leading presenter in the field of education; his message about the importance of teaching has resonated with hundreds of thousands of educators around the world. Todd is a professor of educational leadership at Indiana State University in Terre Haute, Indiana, and he has spent his life pursuing his love of education by researching and studying effective teachers and principals.

Before moving into higher education, he was a math teacher and basketball coach in Missouri; he still holds a school record for most wins in a season at one of the high schools where he coached. Todd then served as a principal at the middle school, junior high, and high school levels. He was also a middle school coordinator in charge of staffing, curriculum, and technology for the opening of new middle schools.

One of the nation's leading authorities on staff motivation, teacher leadership, and principal effectiveness, Todd has written 18 educational books, including the national bestseller *What Great Teachers Do Differently*. Other titles include *Dealing with Difficult Teachers, Teaching Matters, Great Quotes for Great Educators, What Great Principals Do Differently, Motivating & Inspiring Teachers,* and *Dealing with Difficult Parents.*

Todd is married to Beth, also a former teacher and principal, who is a professor of elementary education at Indiana State University. They are the parents of three children: Katherine, Madeline, and Harrison.

Acknowledgements

I would like to thank my wife Beth, my sister Reverend Rene' Whitaker, and Celia Bohannon. Without each of your efforts during the writing, refining, and editing of the manuscript we would never had had a book.

Increase your chances for success . . .

Implementation Guide

Leading School Change:
Nine Strategies to Bring *Everybody* On Board

The interactive **Implementation Guide** provides questions and prompts to assist you and the members of your team to better understand the concepts presented in this book. Also included is a *Quick Start Step-by-Step Action Plan,* a practical tool to help you and your team get started today on implementing change.

Contents

Introduction

Change is inevitable; growth is optional. I liked this idea the first time I heard it, and now it's one of my favorite sayings. In a rapidly changing world, educators and their leaders must choose growth—for themselves personally and for the organizations they serve—and determine how to achieve that growth. The journey can seem daunting, whether we are following a well-worn path or venturing into new territory. It can help to remember that others have made similar choices and taken similar journeys, and we can learn from them.

Shelves full of books have been written about change in the field of education. Many of these present theories or historical research. Some describe *why* we should change, or—even more directly—prescribe *what* we should be changing in our schools. There's nothing inherently wrong with that approach. But this book is different. It's not about theoretical, historical, or hypothetical changes. It's about real change happening today in real schools.

This book presents nine strategies for managing change effectively. I wrote it chiefly for educational leaders at the school or district level, with examples drawn from my experience working with principals and assistant principals, district superintendents, and other educators who want to foster growth in their domains. I hope everyone who wants his or her school to grow better will read it. The odds of success are greater when everyone—each person on the school improvement team, each member of the curriculum committee, and every teacher working to improve classroom instruction—understands the dynamics of change.

In this book, I won't try to tell you what specific changes to make, or even what types of changes to make. Every setting is different, and you know—or you can figure out—what your organization needs. But I do hope to illustrate how to set realistic goals, plan your approach, and track your progress as you go along. I hope to point out obstacles you should avoid and factors you can tilt in your favor. I hope to help you understand how to work effectively with the people in your setting—those who already support the change you seek, those who dig in their heels to resist change of any kind, and everyone in between.

Managing change in schools is never straightforward. It's much more like playing chess than like playing checkers. If you play checkers often enough, you begin to recognize certain patterns. Furthermore, until a piece advances to the king row, all of your pieces have to march across the board in the same direction. Well, chess players also start each game with a specific set of pieces in specific positions, but each piece moves differently, and the number of possible combinations is so vast that every game can turn into a contest much different from the one before.

Likewise, when we embark on change in a school or school district, we start with a set of people with their own ingrained habits and ways of thinking. If we can get them to work together for a common purpose, we definitely tip the odds in our favor.

And steering change in schools is never easy. Instead of facing an equal opponent across the table, it's more as if we're competing against a supercomputer named "the status quo." This adversary has outlasted many a challenger and seems to have an inherent advantage. As we know, however, the chess masters can still outwit the programmed machines—and even the status quo comes up against the inevitability of change. Our task is to steer that change *in the direction we choose* by applying intentional strategies to maximize the chance of success as the game unfolds.

When I wrote the book *Dealing with Difficult Teachers* (2002), I looked at all the resources I could find. Ironically, their basic message was that school administrators who wanted to improve their schools needed to deal with their difficult teachers. Well, guess what? I already knew that. I wasn't looking for direction. I needed strategies!

As I kept digging, about all I could find was advice on how to formally document the situation (what a deluxe treat that is!) so that over the course of a few years I could accumulate the paperwork needed to dismiss the dead-wood. But in my view, we can't afford to wait a few years to improve our schools. We need to make these essential changes now. Each of us can recognize the need for change. The challenge lies in knowing *how to make it happen*.

This book offers specific strategies to help you effectively implement whatever changes you need to make—strategies that dramatically increase your chances of getting widespread acceptance and implementation of your organization's goals. Following these approaches will put you on the path to improvement—not in a few years, but now.

The strategies in this book are numbered from 1 to 9, but that doesn't mean you have to apply them in that order, or that one is more important than another. In fact, they work together and reinforce each other. You can decide when and where and how to apply them, depending on the specific situations and mix of personalities in your setting. You may focus on one at the start, turn to another that makes sense as a way to get around a particular obstacle, and move on to a third once the road is clear ahead. You may find some of them easier to put into practice than others, and it's fine to start with those. But the ones that come less easily to you might be the very ones that will make you a more effective leader, and the very ones that will make the difference between success and failure in your setting.

As you try out these nine strategies and learn how to pursue them more effectively, you may be able to reflect on past efforts and see why some never got off the ground, some went well, and some fizzled out. You may even decide to try again in some area where success has eluded you, putting your new tools to work.

Don't expect to master these strategies on the first attempt, but don't give up on them, either. I have every confidence that after a time, you will be able to look back and say with satisfaction, "There, and there, and there I see growth." And then keep moving forward on the journey.

Good luck and good reading!

Strategy 1
Identify the Change

| 1 | 2 | 3 | 4 | 5 | 6 | 7 | 8 | 9 |

In my high school years, I began to take an interest in the dating scene. I even knew who I wanted to ask out. But I didn't know what to say or how to say it, and I lacked the confidence to figure it out on my own. In the end, I confided in an older friend. Her first question was, "What kind of date?"

She went on to explain that if it was a study date, I could start by talking about a particular homework problem and then say, "Do you want to meet in the library after school?" If it was a group date, I could just say "A bunch of us are going to play miniature golf on Saturday. Would you like to come along?" She said, "Don't start with the prom as your first date; you have to work up to that."

This book won't attempt to solve your love life, but I do hope to provide some specifics that will enable you to move your school toward its goals. And one of the first steps is to decide where you want to go. This may seem simplistic, but the path to change begins with clearly identifying the change you want to make.

What's Your Problem?

I have had the good fortune of working with numerous leaders in a variety of professions. Sometimes the work is in leading change; other times it involves personal skill development or improving staff morale. I recently helped a few employers look at issues involving workforce motivation. One leader wanted to discuss an employee about whom he had major concerns.

"What's the problem?" I asked. "Absenteeism," he responded. I asked again, "Well, what's the problem?" He gave the same answer: "Absenteeism." I asked one more time, "What's the real problem?" (You can see why I am in such demand as a consultant!)

I then explained that the employee's absenteeism was a symptom, not a problem. Was she simply missing too much time at work? Or was her work unsatisfactory even when she was at her desk? Before we decided on a course of action, we needed to identify the goal. Did he want to get her to work every day, or did he want to track the number of days she missed as a way to justify letting her go? Only when we knew the goal could we come up with a solution.

The same principle applies in any setting. Is the challenge to raise reading scores, or to improve reading? Or do you need to do both? Is the problem that your school isn't safe, or that people do not feel safe at school? Do you need a new written discipline policy, or do you simply want to improve student behavior? Does the school community fail to value your teachers, or is the problem that they don't *feel* valued? Do you want to implement professional learning communities, or is the goal really to help each student succeed, with PLCs as one tool for that purpose? I can't answer these questions for you, but it is essential to answer them before moving forward.

Also, you need to determine exactly who will be affected by your decisions. Is this change for one grade level? For a department or team within the school? For the whole school? For the entire district? Be sure to consider not only the direct effects, but also the repercussions. If you start the school day with an assembly to improve school spirit, will lunch periods be more rushed or crowded? If you allow students to eat lunch outdoors, will you need additional monitors? If you spend more time on reading, will there be less time for math or for music?

Another variable to consider is the source or impetus for the change you seek. Sometimes, this is change that the people within your organization need or want. More and more often, however, it seems that changes are imposed from outside. You can raise the odds of achieving success if you take this factor into account as you move forward.

Three Levels of Change

Those shelves full of books written about change include many approaches to the subject. Some authors describe first-order and second-order change; others differentiate among developmental, transitional, and transformational change; still others specify different subsets. Each of these has its place, and all are probably more sophisticated than my view. For our purposes, I'd like to look at three levels of change: procedural, structural, and cultural.

Now, these terms may seem complex, but their definitions are straightforward. As you read about the three levels of change, please keep in mind that in general people view any change—even something as trivial as someone else parking where they ordinarily park—as a big deal. However, defining these levels can help us more effectively lead change in our own settings. Figure 1 illustrates these three levels of change.

Procedural Change

A procedural change involves a very low-level or technical alteration, often a change in procedure (hence the name). Here are a few examples:

- Instead of having teachers take attendance at the start of the class period, have them do so at the end.
- Change the fire drill plan so that students assemble by home room instead of by grade level.
- Instead of always sending students to the lunch line in the same order by class, rotate the order weekly.

Typically, a procedural change is so simple that you could use a memo to inform people, although we know bet-

Figure 1
Three Levels of Change

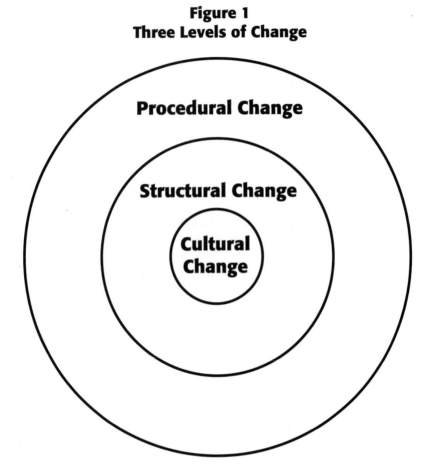

ter than to rely on a memo to inform people of any change, no matter how simple or complex!

I have described these procedural changes as *simple,* but that is not to say they are *easy.* Keep in mind that even minimal changes can become big deals if they are not handled with care.

Structural Change

Although more complex than a procedural change, a structural change is still a matter of management or organization. Examples include:

- Introducing a block schedule at a high school.
- Switching to new textbooks for all of the math programs at a middle school.
- Increasing all class sizes in a district due to budget cuts.

Each of these requires a change in the structure of an organization, but it does not inherently lead to a change in *people*. Sure it does, you may say, it ticks them off! Well, maybe, but structural change doesn't necessarily change *the way people do things*. If a high school class meets for 90 minutes every other day instead of 50 minutes every day, the teacher may just hand out nine worksheets in a period instead of five; the worksheet-to-minute ratio stays the same, and so does her instructional approach. Issuing new textbooks doesn't mean a teacher will adopt new ways of teaching math. Changing the organizational structure doesn't necessarily alter the dynamics within a classroom.

When we get to the third level of change we may find this all easier to understand.

Cultural Change

Cultural change involves *how we do things* in an organization, a more challenging and complex undertaking by far. When we change the culture, we change the very soul and spirit of the group.

Let's look at a classic example: A school community decides, "From now on, we will make all of our decisions based on what is best for our students." This may mean changing the way attendance is taken (a procedural change); it may mean changing the schedule (a structural change); and if the school determines, for example, that more hands-on instruction leads to better learning, it will mean *changing the way teachers teach*.

Wait a minute—won't that involve a lot of extra work? Yes, cultural change is difficult. It often triggers resistance. It may be flat-out scary, precisely because of the extra work. Getting anyone, much less everyone, to change their approach to teaching and learning is a daunting task, but it can be done. Once the cultural change is accomplished and every decision is based on what is best for students, the school community may find it much easier to implement future procedural and structural changes.

Making Sense of the Levels of Change

Many schools are in the process of implementing professional learning communities (PLCs), which bring a school's teachers and administrators together to identify and implement ways to improve student learning. Now ask yourself this question: What level of change does that represent? I'm not sure what your answer will be; I'd guess either structural or cultural. When I survey a large group of educators, these are the most common responses. However, the answer is really a little muddled.

If you mandate the implementation of PLCs, this represents a structural change. You can set up common meeting times and put together a PLC handbook, complete with instructions and directives of what should take place within a learning community. You can achieve the structural change, and you can pay lip service to its value. But getting people to actually follow through is not quite so easy. If the new approach is to have any true meaning, people have to change their behavior. That requires a cultural change: quite a different challenge.

I facilitate quite a few leadership team conferences at which several educators from a school or district work together to develop an "action plan" for change. Some teams attend the workshop with goals already in mind; others develop them on site. As one of the first activities, I ask them to specify the changes they want to make and discuss what level of change each represents. Typically, their responses include each of the three categories. That makes sense: some outcomes are procedural in nature, others structural or cultural. As we continue, however, teams often realize that effectively implementing a structural or even a procedural change will depend on improving the culture. Here is an example.

> A leadership team decides that the school should implement a new discipline code. Perhaps teachers feel that student behavior is inappropriate; perhaps parents have raised concerns; perhaps the district or state has issued new requirements. At first, the team may describe this as a structural change. Their plan may call for changing the number of tardies before a student gets a detention, specifying a different length of suspension for students who fight, or implementing new procedures for passing from one class to another. Obviously, the team needs to make logical and reasonable decisions about these details. But perhaps one reason the leadership team is addressing the issue at all is that their school really needs to make a cultural change.

> What is the outcome they seek? Is their goal to have a new discipline code, or is it to improve student behavior? The difference between these two questions may be the difference between a structural change and a cultural change. Recall that a cultural change involves *how we do things*. Potentially, introducing a new discipline code requires little or no change in the behavior of the *adults* in the school (except maybe the assistant principal who doles out the consequences for infractions). However, improving student behavior may be another matter.

As we all know, the key to improving student behavior lies in improving the way adults throughout the school community—teachers, administrators, staff members, bus drivers, and others —interact with students. This means *changing the way we do things*—and that is a cultural change!

Two Major Assumptions

As we move forward into the other strategies for creating and sustaining change, I would like to highlight two assumptions that underpin this book. The first is that the most challenging kind of change to make is cultural change. If your school culture declares that you make decisions based on what is best for students, it *should* be relatively easy to implement structural or procedural changes; all you have to do is demonstrate that the changes meet the criterion, and all staff should come on board. But few organizations have such a strongly established positive culture, and so in most cases the outcomes you seek require cultural change. With that in mind, as you read this book, I ask you to focus on implementing change at the cultural level. If you can learn that art, the knack of managing structural and procedural change should follow.

The other assumption I'd like to emphasize is that if you take the right approach from the start, the effects begin to take hold rather quickly. You may hear elsewhere that it takes five years or more to change an organization's culture. Well, we don't have five years to make our schools more effective. We need to do it now. We may not make significant changes in five minutes, but surely we can do it in five weeks or five months. Let me share one example of how fast a culture can start to change.

Think about the culture that develops around the dinner table as a family eats together every night, or once a week, or even less. Certain patterns take hold: where people sit, who prepares the food, who clears the table, who may be excused and when. Even the conversation (or lack thereof) has a definite rhythm, with the same people doing most of the talking and the same topics discussed or never brought up.

Now think about what happens when company comes. Someone gets bumped into a different seat. Conversation flows in a different direction, with certain topics perhaps more taboo. No matter how established that dinner-table culture, one new person can alter the dynamics. If that person comes often and has a strong influence, the new dynamics may take hold for a while, maybe for a long while, and maybe forever. (If you don't believe me at first, just think about what happens when a new baby comes into the family!)

Set Your Sights High

Are there lessons we can learn from this? Yes, indeed. Set your sights high. Understand that improving our class-rooms and our schools means improving the skills and maximizing the efforts of all the people who work there. Once you have identified your goals for significant change, you and your team can get to work. Together, you can begin to make a difference.

Strategy 2

Make Sure the First Exposure Is Great!

1	**2**	3	4	5	6	7	8	9

In my experience, one consistent obstacle to effective change is the failure to ensure a strong start. I have worked with hundreds of organizations and belong to many more, and by now, when I watch someone plant the first seed of an idea, I almost always know whether it has a good chance of sprouting. Therefore, the second of our nine strategies for change highlights the fact that a strong start lays the essential foundation for growth.

The New Restaurant

The most popular start-up business in the United States is an eatery. There are all types of restaurants: elegant places with fancy menus, mom-and-pop diners, fast-food franchises, and everything in between. Some explode with success and branch out exponentially. Others are quietly shuttered just a few months down the road. In fact, the business most likely to fail is also an eatery. What goes wrong?

Of course, a number of factors affect how well a restaurant does. First of all, many of the folks who start one know little about running a restaurant. (We've had that experience in education: Everyone went to school, so everyone thinks she or he is an expert at running one!) People who have eaten at a variety of places believe they can do as well, or better, but most of the time they miss the mark. The fortunate few have to get everything right: prices, competition, menu choices, appearance, location, service, and so on. But one factor that goes a long way toward determining a start-up's success is the public's first exposure to the eatery.

Isn't it exciting when a new restaurant opens up near you? You watch the construction or renovation. You see that first "Help Wanted" sign and the notice posting the hours. The grand opening finally arrives, you make your first visit, and your anticipation turns to disappointment. The place is crowded—which should be a good sign— but the kitchen can't keep up, and clearly the cook hasn't worked out all of the kinks for some recipes.

The owners may think, "The first week didn't go too well, but we'll iron things out." However, many customers won't give the place a second chance, and as they talk about their experience, others may not even make that first visit.

Does this mean the new eatery has no chance? Of course not. But the owners have wasted their best chance. It takes eight times longer to unlearn something than it does to learn it in the first place. In other words, diners who had a bad experience would have to return for several enjoyable meals in order to overcome their first impression.

By contrast, many new restaurants start with private openings for invited guests. They practice several times with a hand-picked full house and refine their procedures before opening to the public. They strive to build goodwill by making sure their customers' first exposure is great. We can draw a direct parallel between this and the experience of introducing change in schools.

No Child Left Behind

Discussing the merits or limitations of the No Child Left Behind Act is a conversation with no end. The program has a host of entrenched opponents. One factor that got it off to a poor start, I believe, was the way it was introduced to educators. In many instances, someone from the Department of Education (and perhaps not the most skilled spokesperson) presented the program's expectations and consequences in a manner that educators perceived as threatening. Often, the message came across as: "We have tried to tell you too many times! You need to be better at teaching everyone, and if you aren't, then watch out. We are finally going to hold your feet to the fire! Coming down the pike is this new program called No Child Left Behind..."

Now, NCLB may have generated disdain for several other reasons, but certainly in many settings the initial negative tone stirred up resistance that its advocates will never overcome. Many change programs that get off on the wrong foot accumulate so much baggage that they have to start over, recycling their ideas under a new name.

Introducing change is like introducing a new leader: The first impression is all-important. The initial tone, the manner, the personal connections, the ability to build a relationship before it is needed all make a difference. When your leadership team embarks on change (whether it be procedural, structural, or cultural) you must plan ahead to make the initial exposure as positive as possible.

Effective teachers do this at the start of each school year. They understand that the first day, the first interaction with new students, sets the expectations for the rest of the year. Will it be a constant power struggle or a productive adventure? The first exposure is what makes the difference.

But I'm Excited! Won't Everyone Else Be Excited Too?

Who among us hasn't returned from a professional conference or workshop all fired up about a new idea or program introduced by an excellent speaker? Our first exposure was great, and we're excited to have our colleagues and organization adopt, say, project-based learning. So we rush back and start to spread the word about the greatest new thing since sliced bread. Somehow our enthusiasm doesn't catch on the way we thought it would. Some colleagues respond with indifference, others with negativity. Some may even complain or vigorously object. What on earth happened?

Well, you attended a session with a dynamic and professional presenter who gave you a great first exposure to project-based learning, for example. You may be a little more of a risk taker than some of your colleagues, and you bought into the idea. Others in the room may have already attended a workshop on the idea; if they're back for more information, they probably shared your impression. You may have assumed that your colleagues would respond with equal enthusiasm, but you didn't have the PowerPoint or the speaker's expertise and flair. You didn't even have the introductory jokes that paved the way for your acceptance of project-based learning.

Have you ever heard a hilarious joke on a late-night talk show and tried to tell it to a friend the next day? Sometimes it just doesn't sound quite as funny. Why? First of all, you're not a professional comedian with years of experience telling jokes. You don't have cue cards to ensure that you use exactly the right wording and pause in just the right spot, and you don't have an assistant flashing a neon sign—Laugh!—at the end of each punch line.

But if you had a hard time retelling that joke, think about what happens when your buddy tries to pass it on. It's like the old-fashioned game of Telephone, where a whispered message passes from one person to another—by the time it comes full circle, the message is completely different. "Why do firemen wear red suspenders? To keep their pants up!" may have morphed into "What color suspenders do firemen wear? Red!"

The same thing can happen when you bring a new idea to your colleagues. The message gets diluted as it spreads. Some folks may even put a negative spin on it—"You'll never guess what they are going to make us do now!"

A school can't send all of its staff members to every conference, of course. And we do often expect those who attend professional development sessions to share what they learned with their peers. But second-hand exposure may not facilitate change as effectively as we would hope. What can we do to better the odds?

The Intentional Exposure

Often, people come to my workshops with ideas for change already drafted. Other times, the goals are generated on site. Either way, right from the start I ask participants to make a commitment: They will not pull out their cell phones during breaks and report on the workshop to their colleagues back home. I caution them that even when they get back to their organization, they should take care about how they communicate new concepts to others. Just as great teachers are intentional about how their room is arranged, how they greet students, and even how children use the pencil sharpener, effective leaders of school change practice intentionality every step of the way.

Guest Speakers

Legendary New York Yankees manager Casey Stengel used to describe a baseball team as three groups of players: "those who love you, those who hate you, and a bunch sitting on the fence." The key, he said, was to keep the ones who hate you away from the ones on the fence! Likewise, every school has a few teachers who resist almost every change, a few who support almost every change, and a bunch in the middle. Once the fence-sitters choose a side, they are likely to stay there for the entire game (or even a double-header). Thus, we want to win over as many as possible as quickly as we can. One way to do that is to have an outside speaker or consultant provide the first exposure to your idea.

If you intend to introduce project-based learning, for example, you'll have an easier time if you get people believing in it from the start. It's much harder to convert opponents into proponents. (Remember, it takes eight times longer to unlearn something than it does to learn it in the first place.) Bringing in an advocate for the change you seek—a professional with expertise and flair—sets you up for success.

Site Visits

If you decide to visit schools that have already effectively implemented a change you would like to introduce, practice intentionality. Make sure you know what your staff members will see on the visit. Don't randomly choose three schools that just happen to be doing project-based learning; visit sites where excellent teachers will share positive experiences. If the first exposure is less than convincing, it will take much more time, money, and effort to overcome that initial impression.

Also think carefully about who makes the trip. Don't view early site visits as a chance to win over those who might oppose your plan. Realize that the first people to go to another site will become your resident experts. They will see the plan in action and know how it works. You want the forerunners to come back and share predominantly positive feedback about the change you intend to introduce. In other words, send people who have expressed openness to change, and be sure to organize an opportunity for that crucial first exposure on the home front.

What happens if your first visiting crew includes a couple of negative members? In the worst-case scenario, they will spread the wrong message, even if they don't do so in public. "A lot of the teachers I visited said that we should stay clear of project-based learning. It's way more work for the teacher, and the students hate it."

Does this mean that you never send negative staff members on a school visit? No, obviously this would not be an appropriate long-term approach at all. But you don't have to send them in the early crews; wait until after the positive messages take hold. And you don't have to send them with other naysayers; a van full of generally positive people may influence the less optimistic person to have a more open mind. One way to do this is to send the positive-minded ones first and have some of them return as tour guides on your next visit.

Staff Meetings

If you intend to introduce an idea for change at a staff meeting, set the stage carefully for an upbeat and constructive tone. In the book *Dealing with Difficult Teachers* (2002), I include drawings that show where the more negative and resistant staff members tend to cluster at staff meetings: in the back of the room or near the door. It's almost as if this area is emotionally "reserved" for them.

If this happens in your setting, I would encourage you to "shuffle the deck." At the very least, remove extra chairs to establish physical closeness, and turn them so the front podium is near the door. You can (discreetly) ask administrators and other individuals who have a good influence to sit beside some of the more vocally negative folks; this might make them more subdued and less likely to roll their eyes at their cronies every time you mention the idea of improving your school.

Even if you can't set the stage like this on a permanent basis, be sure to do so now and then, and particularly before meetings at which you hope to win support for change. (You don't want to do it *only* then, however, because people might focus on the furniture arrangement rather than the content of your message.)

In addition to the staff meeting, you might hold a series of small-group sessions for the crucial first exposure, starting with the more positive potential supporters and gradually bringing in the fence-sitters. Again, be intentional about the makeup of these groups. Effective teachers think carefully when setting up small-group work, especially when there are more challenging students in the mix. Such intentionality is equally important, maybe even more important, when working with adults to build support for change.

Don't Bring Up the Negatives

There is a reason theatres show the best parts of a movie in the preview trailer. Whether the funniest bits of a comedy or the scariest scene of a thriller, these teasers are designed to present the most appealing parts of the upcoming feature flicks. Conversely, the slower or more boring segments don't make it into the previews. The movie promoters know that if your first exposure is not enticing, you're unlikely to come back for the whole show!

The same reasoning applies to the crucial first exposure to an upcoming change in your school. Almost every new concept has some potential drawbacks. A school that increases the time for reading and writing will have to limit other learning opportunities; many new programs will require more effort and resources; modifying a procedure involves a learning curve. You will have many occasions to discuss and evaluate the pros and cons of the upcoming change. Nevertheless, the first exposure should highlight only the positives.

This does not mean that you should distort the facts or hide the downsides. In fact, you must be prepared to discuss potential drawbacks or provide more specifics if someone asks a question or raises a concern. At the very least, be ready to acknowledge that some aspects need further attention. A comment such as "We will make sure to explore that issue" can take the edge off someone's apprehensions. Use caution so that stumbling blocks don't turn into roadblocks before you even get started.

It makes sense to take the time to prepare for questions and concerns that may arise in the early stages. That's another reason not to rush back from a conference or workshop all fired up about an idea and trumpeting its benefits. Let it settle—that positive first exposure is worth waiting for.

How Important Is the First Exposure?

High viewer ratings for the pilot of a prospective new television show may not necessarily portend a new hit series, but they sure don't hurt. By the same token, an initial staff meeting that comes off with flying colors doesn't guarantee success, and a meeting that goes badly doesn't doom the intended change to failure, but by taking the extra steps to set up a positive first exposure, you can improve the odds for effective change in your schools.

Strategy 3

Determine Who Matters Most

| 1 | 2 | **3** | 4 | 5 | 6 | 7 | 8 | 9 |

As we set out to improve the dynamics in our organization, we need to understand the makeup of the people in the group. This understanding helps with every task of leadership, but it is critical when change is on the agenda.

Now of course we recognize that every employee in a school is important. When we embark on change, however, we must figure out which of our employees are *essential* and how to make the most of these key players. Their support paves the way to wider acceptance and buy-in for our goals. Even before we start planning for a strong first exposure, we must determine who matters most.

Three Types of Employees

I'm convinced that one of the essential components— if not *the* essential component—of leading change is to understand the informal dynamics of a group. There are many ways to break these down. Dr. Al Burr (1993), a former school administrator, offered a valuable perspective on teacher dynamics. He divided employees into three groups: Superstars, Backbones, and Mediocres. In the book *Six Types of Teachers* (2005), Fiore and Whitaker sort these into three similar categories, each with two subcategories. Their main groupings are the Irreplaceables, the Solids, and the Replacement Level.

Each of these groupings will apply in any profession. In a restaurant, you will find three types of wait staff; at the hospital, three types of medical professionals; at a bank, three types of tellers and three types of loan officers. The catego-

ries also apply to other staff members in a school district—
bus drivers, cooks, custodians, and guidance counselors,
as well as principals and assistant principals. However, for
the purpose of understanding the dynamics, let's examine
the categories as they apply to teachers.

Superstars / Irreplaceables

To reach the lofty level of the irreplaceable superstar, a
teacher must earn the esteem of four groups: students, parents, peers, and principals.

- If you ask students to name their best teachers, this
  teacher's name comes up quite often.
- Parents often request (or at least wish) that their child
  have this teacher. The word gets around the school
  community that his classroom serves the needs of
  students well.
- Peers respect this teacher as a colleague, role model,
  and informal leader.
- If this teacher left the school, the principal would find
  it difficult to hire someone as good, and the departure
  would matter beyond the walls of her classroom.

A lofty standard indeed, but this is truly a rare group of
professionals. In a typical organization, about 2 to 10 percent of employees count as irreplaceable. In a school, you
might find one or two superstars—if you're lucky, a handful to a dozen. That's pretty heady stuff.

Backbones / Solids

Backbones typically make up 80 to 90 percent of an organization. There are lots of different ways to think of this
group; perhaps the easiest is this. If two or three backbones
left our school, we would most likely break even in replac-
ing them. Sometimes we would do a little better, sometimes
a little worse. That doesn't mean that there wouldn't be chal-

lenges. We may think, "Where are we going to find someone who can teach high school biology *and* coach junior varsity girls' volleyball?" Or "Who can we get to sponsor Student Council—no one likes to do that!"

Some of these backbones rank among our most supportive faculty members. Further, they do much of the work in our organization simply because they comprise such a large percentage of the staff. As individuals, the solids might have some characteristics we would greatly miss, along with some quirks or traits that we could easily do without. They may even have some of the traits needed to be a superstar or irreplaceable, but they come up short in at least one area to qualify for that category.

Mediocres / Replacement Level

Our mediocre employees hold down the other end of the bell-shaped curve from the superstars—typically 5 to 10 percent of our faculty and staff. This is the teacher parents probably don't prefer for their child; this is the secretary who tends to arrive late and leave early; this is the coach who typically blames the refs when the team doesn't win. In short, if a mediocre left, we could easily find someone better to fill that slot.

There's nothing mean-spirited about recognizing this fact. And since the *if* is a big *if*—because given their shortcomings, they're not likely to find a better job offer at another school—we will need to work with them in our setting to lead change effectively. Examples of these employees appear in scenarios later in the book, and we'll explore approaches to dealing with them under Strategy 8, *Reinforce Changed Behaviors*.

What Does This Mean to My Organization?

Recognizing where you have an abundance of talent and identifying your potential weaknesses is a crucial step to moving forward. We will save the details for a later time, but outlining a few characteristics of employee types now can help you understand the dynamics they create no matter where they work. You may want to spend a few minutes to identify which people in your setting fit into each category and then make a list of adjectives that describe the individuals in each of these groups. Over the years, I have found that people come up with similar responses. Typical lists include the following:

- Superstars / Irreplaceables — good communicator, initiator, visionary, risk taker; caring, positive, knowledgeable, energetic, creative, dynamic; has a sense of humor, loves teaching, puts students first.
- Backbones / Solids — hard worker; dedicated, loyal, productive, knowledgeable, consistent; follows directions, likes teaching, tries hard.
- Mediocres / Replacement Level — slacker, cynic; negative, incompetent, sarcastic; resists change, knows the contract word for word, has poor attendance record, lacks classroom management skills.

At one workshop, a principal noted that the backbone group could have all the qualities of the superstar if we just added "for the most part." In other words, they are positive most of the time, generally put students first, and so on. We'll see examples of these dynamics at work in our schools as we explore additional strategies. However, here I'd like to highlight a couple of reasons that we must have a clear view of these dynamics. They involve two critical differences among our groups of mediocres, backbones, and superstars.

How Broad Is Their Vision?

Think about the superstars in your organization. How broad is their vision? In my experience, the irreplaceable teachers take in the whole setting. In everything they do, in every decision they make, they envision its effects throughout the school. They may even consider the district-wide, statewide, or worldwide impact.

How broad is the vision of the backbones in your organization? In my experience, it is often limited by their classroom walls. The solid teachers consider decisions and view potential changes in terms of how it will directly affect them, their teaching practices, and their students.

How broad is the vision of the mediocres in your organization? As big as a mirror: They think of themselves. Replacement-level teachers typically make decisions and respond to change by asking, "What difference does this make for me?" Not "for my students" or "for my department" or "for my grade level," but "What does it mean for me?"

Of course, not every individual in each of these categories always thinks this way, but this is the vision that tends to set their horizons. Once we recognize these differences, we can take them into account as we make decisions and manage the everyday routine. They become crucially important as we seek to implement change. So too does one other essential difference among the groups: the locus of the impetus for change.

Where Is the Impetus for Change?

Where does the impetus for change come from in each of these groups? In my experience, superstars have an internal impetus for change. They monitor their practices to get a sense of whether they work. If this reflection suggests that another approach might work better, they adjust accordingly.

Backbones, on the other hand, have an external impetus for change. Typically, they need an outside force to nudge them toward a different approach. They adjust when they are strongly encouraged or required to do so, and they may initially resist. Seldom do they generate change on their own.

By the way, schools operate in a similar way. In a study of 700 schools (Turner, 2002) that compared test scores predicted using socioeconomic status with actual test results, schools that exceeded their predicted scores were found to have an internal impetus for change. And this extended beyond change related to curriculum and instruction. If they were dissatisfied with the flow of lunch lines, for example, or hallway traffic, or carpool pick-up and drop-off procedures, they tweaked the system until it ran smoothly. This contrasted markedly with schools that underperformed their predicted levels. Lagging schools made changes only when given external motivation, such as a new board policy, a change in state or federal mandates, or requirements imposed by the superintendent. This variation between high-achieving and low-achieving schools parallels the difference between superstars and backbones.

What about the mediocres? We often describe these replacement-level teachers as resistant to change or improvement. In my view, however, it's more accurate to call them resistant to hard work. They prefer to go with the flow, even if it's downhill. Indeed, if improvement required less effort than their current practices, some of them would be all over it. And as we'll see when we come to Strategy 6, *Harness the Power of Emotion,* they tend to welcome change if it makes their own situation better.

Six Types of Teachers

I mentioned earlier that in the book *Six Types of Teachers* (2005), Fiore and Whitaker refine these three groups by developing subgroups. Understanding the subgroups may help us implement change more effectively.

The Superstars / Irreplaceables
    WOW (walks on water)—the role model
    Impacter—great in the classroom

The Solids / Backbones
    Stabilizer—solid at everything
    Dow Joneser—pluses and minuses

Replacement Level / Mediocres
  Harmless—no complaints, little benefit
  Negative Force—addition by subtraction

The superstar / irreplaceable teachers fall into two sub-groups, typically distinguished by how outgoing they are outside the classroom. One group is called the WOWs (the ones who *walk on water*). Known for being outstanding in the classroom, these teachers are also natural leaders. They are usually very gregarious, and they have a broad influence among their peers. If they think something is a good idea, they tout it widely, typically pulling many others onto the bandwagon.

The teachers in the impacters subgroup are equally good in the classroom—maybe even better, though not nearly as many people are aware of it. Colleagues who have taught with them know and respect their work, as may a few others, but these teachers are less in the limelight than the WoWs. If they think something is a good idea, it almost always is, but they are less likely to use their influence to convince their peers. They are also less likely to want to be in the forefront of change.

Solids / backbones can also be divided into two sub-groups. The stabilizers are strong and steady, although rarely spectacular. The energy thermostat in their classroom stays set at 68 degrees. Tuesday is like Friday, November is like April. They handle high-achieving students, average children, and struggling learners with pretty much the same aplomb. Not many students would name these as favorite teachers, but almost no one would speak negatively of them. When it comes to change, they are willing to try almost anything without complaining about it. They do not seek to influence others, but if they look askance at an idea it will raise a cautionary flag for some of their peers.

Now, the Dow Jonesers (as legendary basketball announcer Dick Vitale called inconsistent players) are a different story—a story of ups and downs. Their enthusiasm for a task can raise their performance to star quality, but they may well run out of steam. If you can surround them with dynamic people they'll seem charged up, but in a humdrum situation their performance may be lackluster. Their classroom energy thermostat swings from 80 degrees one day to a chilly 60 the next. They work well with students they like, not so well with others. When it comes to change, you want them on board, and they may jump on the bandwagon right away. However, you can't rely on their consistent support.

Finally, replacement level / mediocres have two subgroups as well. The ones we call harmless earn that potentially misleading label because they stop short of being negative forces. Students learn very little in their classrooms, but they are not damaged in the process—no aha! moments, but no scar tissue. These teachers get through the day and the year without making waves. When it comes to change, they will neither lead nor block the way; they may simply get out of the way. They don't throw a fit when the new textbooks arrive; they just clear a space for them on the shelf where the old ones stood. The harm they do by letting change flow past their classrooms may go unnoticed.

Negative force staff members not only resist change, they fight it. They may fight it vocally in a public forum, but they have also mastered the technique of griping and sniping behind the scenes. Their negativity leaves its traces in the classroom, the teachers' workroom, and wherever else they go. The phrase "addition by subtraction" underscores the fact that if they leave the school, the situation improves. When it comes to change, we must recognize these individuals as potential roadblocks and figure out how to work with them in order to contain the damage, or work around them to reach our goals.

Who Matters Most?

Of these six groups of people, who matters most when it comes to implementing change? Surely we don't want to let the negative forces hold sway. Nor can we afford to focus our time and energy on jump-starting the resistant mediocres. We can rely on the backbones, more so on the stabilizers than the Dow Jonesers, but the ones who matter most are the irreplaceable teachers. These superstars have the broadest vision of what the change will mean, and they have the internal motivation to move forward. The WOWs are natural leaders with substantial influence among their peers. They will be the vanguard of change. Let's make sure we understand what makes them tick, and how to make the most of it.

Understanding the Irreplaceables / Superstars

One trait often attributed to superstars is that they are "born to teach." I personally find this comment out of line, because it seems to imply that they were just handed a particular gift and all they have to do is let it roll. What if one of your superstars left the field of education to manage a McDonald's franchise? That fast-food site might well become the best-run McDonald's in the state. Would other franchise managers say the superstar was "born for the fast-food industry"?

In my view, superstars generally work harder than anyone else in the organization. It's not that they were born to teach; they have a higher level of talent and drive than most other people. Fortunately for us, they have chosen to apply it to teaching.

What else makes the superstars tick? Two factors come to mind: They thrive on autonomy, and they appreciate recognition.

Today's educational landscape does not always lend itself to fostering a superstar teacher's autonomy. Schools have become highly research driven, and for good reason, but it can be overdone. Some educational settings want research to support every change. That can cramp the style of a creative and innovative educator. If our superstars are on the cutting edge, breaking new ground, there is no research on their methods—because nobody has tried them before. If we see that happening in our schools, we need to take the shackles off and then start the research by observing the innovative teachers.

Among the constraints holding back the best teachers is standardized testing. The tests don't reward creativity or measure the best that superstars can achieve in the classroom. Teachers are much less likely to teach three-digit addition if the test stops at two places. A follower will never cure cancer, but there is at least a chance that a risk taker might. We must make sure that we do not hold a superstar back.

As mentioned, these irreplaceable staff members also appreciate recognition. They don't necessarily crave public events with plaques or trophies or a teacher-of-the-year award. However, they do need acknowledgment that their performance goes above and beyond the standard work of others in their profession. It is important to strike the right balance so that superstars are not perceived as the "principal's pet."

This brings up a related point. In laying out Strategy 2, *Make Sure the First Exposure Is Great!,* we mentioned the tactic of breaking up clusters of negativity at staff meetings by asking a few individuals who have a positive influence to sit next to some of the more vocal naysayers. Here it's the reverse: You should take care not to diminish the power and influence of superstars by habitually sitting next to them at meetings, which might give the impression of favoritism. But you can and should include them in the vanguard as you move toward your goals.

You Don't Have to Guess

Part of this process involves using the key players to screen your plans and proposals right from the start. If the superstars do not think something is a good idea, what are the odds that it is going to fly with the rest of the faculty? Even more important: what are the chances that it actually *is* a good idea? The superstars are not focusing on how the proposed change will affect them or their classrooms; they are looking at it from the vantage point of the whole school. Their breadth of vision is valuable.

The best part is that you don't have to guess what they think. You can just ask them, because these irreplaceable teachers have another gift: the ability to look you in the eye and tell you the truth. You can trust them not to spread the word that you asked them. Superstars don't feed the rumor mill; that's another trait that earns them the respect of their peers.

People, Not Programs, Make the Biggest Difference

Knowing where to startand identifying the individuals to start with are critical parts of successfully implementing change. The more you understand the people in your organization, the more effectively you can move your school toward its goals.

Strategy 4
Find the Entry Points

1	2	3	**4**	5	6	7	8	9

When we embark on change, one of the challenges is knowing where to start. More specifically, we wonder which of the *people* in our organization we should start with. Should we put our energy into consolidating the support of those already open to change? Could we place one more burden on our busiest staff members? Do we dare ask some of our more negative people to give it a try? Choosing the right entry points and finding the key to open those gates can mean the difference between success and failure.

Start Somewhere, Not Everywhere

Over the years, I have had the good fortune to direct a number of dissertation projects. Their sheer scope and complexity can make the process seem overwhelming. Often, the most daunting moment comes when all the research is done and it's time to start writing. I tell doctoral candidates to jump-start the process by writing just one page—preferably the page they're most eager to write at that moment. It might end up in the middle of the paper or toward the end; they might even delete it in a later revision. However, if they can start with that nugget of one page, at least they are on their way.

The same principle applies to embarking on change. If bringing *everyone* on board seems overwhelming, start with bringing *someone* on board—preferably someone who's likely to be open to the idea.

The Points of Least Resistance

Sometimes our first instinct is to focus on winning over the nonbelievers, those most resistant to the change we seek. Most of the time it's a mistake to follow this instinct. We will discuss the challenge of dealing with the naysayers and foot-draggers in the next chapter, when we explore Strategy 5, *Reduce the Resistance*.

Here we focus on a different strategy: starting with those we expect to offer the *least* resistance. To boost the odds of achieving your goals turn first to the superstars and the new teachers on your staff.

Start with the Superstars

To put it plainly, the superstars will do what it takes to support your efforts, and they will do it exceptionally well. This gets the process off to a strong start and provides solid role models for others. Because the backbones respect the superstars, they will follow their lead. As the program spreads to a wider group of participants, each of them can have the *great first exposure* outlined in Strategy 2.

Vince Lombardi, the legendary coach of the Green Bay Packers, is often quoted as saying, "A chain is only as strong as its weakest link." That can be a powerful motivator, if taken correctly. To improve overall performance, an athlete or a team must work on its weaknesses, not just fine-tune or bulk up its strengths. Tuning your car's engine once a week won't improve your gas mileage if the tires are out of alignment.

As leaders, we must not let our weakest links determine the fate of our organization. We don't want to set the bar for performance at the level of our mediocres. We can't afford to give power to our least productive people. When we embark on change, we must rely on our strongest links— our superstars—to forge the path to success.

Blocking the Burnout

A friend of mine used to repeat the old adage, "If you want to get something done, ask a busy person." He would also declare, "People who say they're burned out probably were never on fire in the first place!" There's a bit of truth—maybe a lot of truth—to each of these statements, and yet we need to exercise caution about overloading one or more of our superstars. Where does the balance lie?

One rule of thumb is to understand that there are some things only our superstars can do and that we must reserve some of their energy for those tasks. This does not mean excusing them from the rotation for supervising recess or the lunchroom. That would set them apart in a way that interferes with the staff's team spirit. It does mean that we ask some of our *backbone* faculty to spearhead less significant change efforts, saving the superstars for when we really need them.

I once served as principal at a large school with three secretaries in the main office: a dynamic superstar, a cheerful stabilizer, and a fairly nice mediocre of the harmless variety. They made a great team. Of course, a river of paperwork flowed through the office. Some was crucial, like the application for a $500,000 grant. Some was repetitive and detail-oriented, but important as day followed day and year followed year. Some was destined for a storage area like the big wooden crate at the end of *Raiders of the Lost Ark*; it had to be done, but it really didn't matter much at all.

Decisions about assigning these responsibilities were almost too obvious. I took care to thank each of the three individually, expressing my appreciation for the work accomplished in that office, but I also took pains not to burn out the superstar with paperwork that the other two could manage just as effectively.

So do ask your superstars to participate in the language arts curriculum group that will determine the educational direction of the school for the next decade. Think twice about the Going Green recycling committee and the bulletin board redecoration task force. True, a superstar could boost the results into magnificence, but that's probably not the wisest use of superstar talent, time, and effort.

Understanding the Odds

One way to make sure we don't isolate any of our superstars is to team them with other staff members whenever possible. When we ask a superstar to complete a task alone, the likelihood of a positive response and a job well done is close to 100 percent. If we pair a superstar and a backbone, the odds of a job well done still approach 100 percent, because the team includes a superstar. Even if we build a team of one superstar and two backbones, or one superstar, one backbone and one mediocre, the odds remain high. Why? Because superstars want to excel, expect to excel, and generally will excel at whatever they try to accomplish. (Of course, we shouldn't push our luck by weighing down the team with naysayers or procrastinators.)

Here's one example. It makes sense to have a superstar attend a workshop on school improvement, then return and present to a group of colleagues. But does it make sense to send three superstars? If we send a "mixed" team, we conserve the energy of the two superstars who stay home. At the same time, we build team spirit among the staff members who do attend.

It's not necessary to include new teachers on these mixed teams, and often they have plenty to do just learning the ropes in a new setting. But when we set out to accomplish specific types of change, we can boost the odds of success considerably by including the "newbies" in the process.

Including the Newbies

A change introduced before new staff members come on board doesn't even look like change to them. It's just another rope to learn, and those relatively new to teaching as a profession won't have old habits to break or established expectations to overcome.

I once served as principal in a single-grade school. Approximately 700 eighth graders—adolescence at its finest!—filled the building. Along with the many drawbacks to a one-grade setting, we experienced certain benefits. For example, if we wanted to implement new lunch-line procedures, we did so at the beginning of a school year, simply spelling them out for that student body. We could make dramatic changes from one year to the next without meeting any more resistance than the same old approach would have triggered. (Of course, there was a certain amount of resistance, no matter what. After all, these were eighth graders.) The key was to make sure that the adults were solidly on board by the start of school—not always an easy task—and that they didn't let on to the students that anything had changed. Ignorance is bliss when it helps people accept a new approach.

The same principle applies to including new staff members in the first round of a startup program. They may not know that the approach has changed, and if they do know, they probably won't care. Again, timing is the key; the program must be ready to roll when the school year starts. Otherwise, rookies and veterans alike must go through a phase of adjustment. Why not take advantage of this opportunity to diminish the impact of change?

Finally, if the new teacher's first encounter with a program occurs during the job interview, there's a strong incentive to say, "Sure, I'd be happy to participate in that!"

Induction Starts with the Interview

The amount of information about teacher induction and the number of programs developed to promote a good start for new hires could fill several filing cabinets. Much of it is valuable, and many of the programs are helpful. However, formal programs often take place at the district level, and almost all of them start in the early fall, *after* the teachers are hired. By contrast, I'm convinced that the best time to introduce expectations and start new teachers on the path you want them to take is during the interview.

The interview situation itself puts candidates in a very cooperative frame of mind, and you know why: They want that job! This is the perfect time to ask, "What would you think about participating in our exchange program? Two or three times a semester, we'll cover your classes while you go observe other teachers who have joined the program. And then we'll cover their classes so they have an opportunity to spend some time in your classroom. Would you consider signing on to this?"

More than at any other point in a teacher's career, the most likely answer is an enthusiastic "Yes!" So why not take advantage of this opportunity to recruit another supporter for change?

Improving Instruction—Together

Sometimes bringing together new staff members and veterans to implement change makes for a perfect fit. Let's say one of your goals is to improve instruction. You have two pathways in mind: having teachers observe in each other's classrooms, and having them videotape and review their own classroom practices for self-directed development. Each of these practices is useful and cost-effective, yet you may find it difficult to integrate them into your school's culture. Let's look at the possibilities for the first pathway when we start with our newest staff members and our best teachers.

Exchanging Visits, Improving Performance

During the school day, our hallways and classrooms bustle with activity. From the moment we enter the building, we are rarely alone. And yet, teaching can be a lonely profession. In many schools, teachers resemble a set of independent contractors connected by some hallways. Although we may always have 25 or so students in the room with us, we seldom interact with our peers during class time. You can begin to overcome this isolation by opening your classrooms to other teachers.

Getting teachers into each others' classrooms while they are teaching is an excellent way to improve instruction and thereby improve a school. If teachers regularly observe their colleagues in a well-organized program, it is likely that each teacher will become more like the best teacher. The reason is simple: Nobody adopts a worse idea. (Nobody attends a professional workshop and concludes, "That won't work as well as what I already do; I think I'll give it a try.") Teachers who voluntarily observe their colleagues in action tend to follow the examples set by the best teachers. However, you must plan carefully as you get this program started.

Plan Ahead and Prepare

Even if your eventual goal is to have all teachers participate, keep in mind the importance of the first exposure. To maximize the odds of success, link the newbies with the best of your current faculty. The key is to plan ahead: by April or May, you typically know whether there will be new hires for the next school year. Here's how your leadership team might roll out this program in a typical scenario.

At a late spring faculty meeting, we let it be known that five new teachers will come on board in the fall. Floating the idea without applying pressure or judgment, we suggest that one way to integrate them into the school community is to pair the rookies with veteran teachers for an exchange of classroom visitations. We do not ask for volunteers right away, in part because it's most likely that only our superstars would raise their hands at this point. While we do hope to launch the program with them, we don't want to single them out in public. (Their peers don't like that, and neither do they.)

We ask for volunteers before summer comes (people are more likely to agree to something if the actual work and effort are months away), and we welcome volunteers from across the spectrum (superstar to mediocre) because eventually we want the program to operate school-wide.

Say that seven current teachers sign on. With five new teachers having agreed to the program during their job interviews, we can be selective about which veterans we start with. We can even take steps to recruit another superstar if need be, and as we'll discuss below, we can carefully lay the groundwork for pairing a newcomer with a less effective teacher.

Good to Go

Our best teachers volunteered last spring, and our new faculty members signed up during the interview, so we are good to go. Early in the fall, we arrange for a substitute, teacher's assistant, or administrator to cover classes so that our volunteers can observe each other at mutually convenient times.

How will it work out? Well, what are the chances that the new staff members will learn something from observing a superstar in action? My guess is about 100 percent. Now the best teachers may also learn something in the exchange. But what are the chances that they will at least *pretend* they learned something from their new colleague, or compliment the rookie for something that went well during the class? My guess is about 100 percent, since one trait of a superstar is professional courtesy.

So for each of these teachers, the first exposure was great. Because of our advance planning, the initial experience for the school was positive. Growing the program will be much easier from this point on, but we need to remain proactive as we expand the number of participants.

Proceed with Caution

Where the superstars lead the way, the backbones will follow. What happens when we start to bring the mediocres on board? We do want them on board, of course. They represent the weakest link in our organization, and this program has great potential for strengthening our overall performance, but before we pair a crusty old mediocre with a new staff member, we must take steps to limit the damage and maximize the gain.

In this situation, I would want to have a conversation along the following lines. One on one with Mr. Newby, I would ask him how the exchange observations have gone. Since he has been paired only with superstars, I would expect a positive response to his first exposure. Next, I would remind him that this program is a mutual exchange. We expect that new teachers can learn from their experienced colleagues and, equally important, that even veteran teachers have room for improvement and can learn from newcomers to their school.

Then ask who Mr. Newby is scheduled to work with next. If the answer is Ms. Downer, a less than positive teacher, I would smile and politely restate my most recent comment: "This program is a mutual exchange." I might go so far as to remind Mr. Newby that he will have opportunities to practice the feedback techniques modeled by the veteran teachers in his previous exchanges.

The key is to get your message across without singling out a less than effective teacher for criticism. You must be able to walk this fine line in order to keep the program going in a positive direction.

Once a few teachers have participated, it becomes easier and easier to bring others on board. Because the first exposures went well, you have advocates for the program in your setting. Gradually involving others is the natural next step.

Inch by Inch, Row by Row

After these successful early exchanges, we may be tempted to require everyone to participate. We will look more closely at moving to full participation when we come to Strategy 7, *Look Past Buy-In to Action*. For now, I'll just comment that it's best not to jump the gun. Rather, I recommend adding people to the mix a few at a time. Without turning away any volunteers, be selective about reeling in those who have not stepped forward.

For example, if two of the four grade 4 teachers have already signed on—and especially if the other two are a new teacher and a superstar—it might be easier to recruit the third and fourth than to start from scratch on the grade 5 level.

When we do move on, it makes sense to continue targeting the points of least resistance. If we approach all three grade 5 teachers at once, they might find it easier to respond with a collective "No." Instead, we could tell Mr. Stabilizer that Ms. Rookie in grade 4 hopes to learn what she should be doing to help her students prepare for next year. Would he be willing to let her observe his classes? And since her first exposure was positive, she's more likely to welcome Mr. Stabilizer's feedback on what he observes in turn. (In fact, if she's confident enough to approach him on her own, all the better.)

Like the graduate student who reduces the daunting task of writing a dissertation to manageable proportions by always working on the section he is most eager to complete, we can build the critical mass by working on one person at a time, always taking the path of least resistance. Once we reach the critical mass, the momentum for change is in our favor.

Self-Directed Development

A good practice that can improve instruction in a school is self-directed development. This is a fancy way of saying that people focus on improvement using goals, logs, plans for growth, diaries, or self-reflection. One way that some schools have accomplished this goal—and one of my favorites—is to have teachers videotape their own classrooms for personal observations. For example, Mr. Oscar signs up to have a class of his choosing recorded by a student, a community volunteer, or another person with whom he feels comfortable. The videotaper enters his room at the appointed time, records the lesson or activity requested, pops out the DVD or tape and quietly leaves the room, handing the only copy to Mr. Oscar. He can then review the session in his own time frame, and since he has the only copy, he can control who else (if anyone) might see it.

Once again, the superstars and new teachers may be the most effective entry points for introducing the practice. Also, inviting individuals to volunteer is more likely to be accepted than announcing that participation is expected. As always, it's important to work out the details for that important first exposure.

To lay the groundwork, you might explore the option of a student camera crew. At almost any grade level, some students are video savvy. Perhaps you can enlist the media center specialist to set up a roster and arrange the scheduling for students and equipment. Once the filming system is in place, you can let teachers know about this option for professional growth.

You could begin with the comment that several faculty members have inquired about taping their own classrooms, and give concrete examples of how this could benefit teachers. Someone applying for National Board Certification might ask to have a lesson recorded. A seasoned teacher taking a graduate course might need documentation of a class project. A science teacher doing a special experiment for the first time might want to review the process before repeating it. Teachers might be curious about whether they call on girls or boys more often, or whether they allow sufficient wait time before expecting students to answer a question.

Rather than asking faculty to indicate interest by raising their hands, you might post a sign-up station online, or in the library, or both. In my experience, the most effective teachers will be among the first to sign up. Furthermore, they are the most likely to follow through: watching the tape, identifying things they could do better the next time, and asking to have the next time recorded as well.

And what about your new teachers? Again, start in the interview. Ask Mr. Candidate what he would think about arranging to have several classes recorded over the next year. Explain that he might choose his best class for a professional portfolio, or one he is struggling with a bit so he can reflect on potential changes, or just a random pick so he can review his performance. Mr. Candidate will most likely say this sounds like a great idea. Why? Well, again, he wants that job!

And when he shows up next fall, remind him about the program and how to sign up. He will assume that this is part of the routine, and there's no reason to tell him otherwise. Just make sure that his first exposure is positive.

From Seedling to Sapling, from Sapling to Tree

As educators, we should know better than to expect change to happen overnight. Growth is incremental. You could start by planting the seed of an idea, helping one or two teachers tape a class or two for their own personal and private reflection. As the practice takes root, each teacher might record a class at least four times a year and share at least one tape with peers for team reflection. As the program grows, many teachers might voluntarily show segments to the principal for suggestions and guidance regarding possible improvements. In time, you might show clips at faculty workshops to show the kind of instruction you strive for. Eventually, your efforts will bear fruit, but not unless you plant the seed and help it grow. To maximize the harvest, you should focus on the points of least resistance.

Strategy 5

Reduce the Resistance

| 1 | 2 | 3 | 4 | **5** | 6 | 7 | 8 | 9 |

Focusing on the easier entry points can take us a long way toward our goals. Working with our superstars and our new teachers is both positive and rewarding, but that doesn't mean we can afford to ignore the resistance we encounter on the path to change. A few negative people with strong personalities will often throw up roadblocks and impede our progress. We know this from the start, of course. Whenever we begin to think and talk about implementing change, these pockets of resistance come to mind. Won't this upset Charlie Crabtree? What do we do about Molly Moper? Will anything get Ben Blockitall to budge?

Unfortunately, it's all too easy to let these obstacles direct the flow. In too many cases, and for far too long, they have obstructed the changes that could improve our schools. We can't eliminate them altogether, but this strategy sets forth a number of ways to reduce the resistance.

Don't Let the Whiners Rule the Roost

The first tactic starts with recognizing that the whiners in our midst are often just plain dissatisfied about everything. They don't like their students. Parents are a hassle. The principal is both "nowhere to be found" and a micromanager—quite a combination! They work way too hard; they get paid way too little. Everything is a conspiracy. As you can imagine, their personal lives aren't going too well either. Bills are piling up; the dog next door barks day and night; they disagree with the preacher at their church. They have car troubles, spouse troubles, weight and health troubles. Whew! No wonder they are miserable. Unfortunately, too often they seem determined to make everyone else unhappy too, and the worst news is they're good at it!

Once we recognize the pattern for what it is, we can treat the whining like background noise. Knowing that they will object to change, we can initiate it anyway. Knowing that they will gripe about work, we can work with them anyway. Knowing that they will focus on the negatives, we can leave that chore to them and focus on the positives. Even though they whine, we can do fine.

Defuse the Drama

In one memorable episode of *The Andy Griffith Show*, Sheriff Andy Taylor's red-headed son Opie makes a new friend, Arnold, who tries to teach him how to manipulate his father and Aunt Bea. As Arnold's dad comes around the corner, the boy drops to the ground and throws a tantrum. His dad rushes over and tries to stop the snuffling and howling. Stroking Arnold's back, he says soothingly, "We'll go get ice cream; we'll go get ice cream." Getting up, Arnold winks knowingly at Opie and struts off for his treat.

Opie heads to the courthouse to try this for himself. When the sheriff enters his office, Opie falls to the floor and throws a (very entertaining) tantrum of his own. Andy basically ignores him—"Well, don't get your clothes all dirty, son"—and gets on with his paperwork. Opie holds his breath until his eyes pop. Andy says, "Yeah, that's good lung exercise."

You can imagine how the scene plays out. Opie's tantrum ends because it didn't work, and it didn't work because Andy refused to be manipulated.

This little narrative may take you back to your own childhood. When Jimmy said, "If I can't be the pitcher, I'll take my ball and go home," you might have let him pitch. When Sally burst into tears because she wanted the first turn on the swing, you might have let her go first. If Jimmy and Sally amped up the volume once or twice, you might have decided that you'd rather let them have their way up front than deal with the drama. If so, they trained you well.

Then they grew up. Now Jimmy teaches geography across the hall from you. He doesn't get his end-of-term paperwork in on time, and the office staff finds it easier to do it for him than to drag it out of him. Sally comes in for parent conferences, pouting and shouting about how her daughter should have had an A in algebra and the lead in the school play. They are still trying to get their way through drama.

But we don't have to let them manipulate us. We grew up too, and we know how to stand our ground. When someone throws a tantrum, we can think to ourselves, "Yeah, that's good lung exercise." By defusing the drama, we can refuse to empower them. We can keep moving toward our goals.

Divide and Conquer

Suppose that five students in Mrs. Malarkey's classroom misbehave as a group. Her first instinct might be to hold all five after class and punish them collectively. That could well backfire. Treating the miscreants as a group can create a bond among them. Even if they weren't really friends when they acted up, they may well be partners in crime from now on, and there is strength in numbers.

If the misbehaving youngsters are in first or second grade, she might consider calling all five sets of parents that very night to enlist their help in quelling their shenanigans. But if the parents are good friends with each other, they may conclude that the "gang of five" is innocent and the problem lies in Mrs. Malarkey's classroom management! It's much more effective to deal with students one at a time, especially as they get older. The goal is to isolate them in their misery and not allow them to reinforce each other's inappropriate behavior.

Now, we can't always extrapolate from managing a classroom to leading change, but this particular example offers a useful tactic for reducing resistance. The trick is to avoid thinking of the naysayers and foot-draggers as a gang to be confronted all at once. It's much more effective to treat them as individuals and win them over one by one. If five teachers oppose the new approach to team teaching, don't think you have to reduce that number to zero in one fell swoop. Take small steps; work on reducing five to four, then three, then two. This tactic makes it easer to persist with Strategy 4 and focus on the points of least resistance.

Effective leaders have a sense of the dynamics in their organization. In a school, these may differ among academic departments or among grade levels. Say all the math teachers resist the new approach to team teaching, while only one in social studies is holding out. Which entry point offers the least resistance and the best odds? Right—the social studies holdout.

When the time does come to tackle the math department, again our tactic is to treat them not as a gang, but as individuals. There may be one negative leader and several less adamant followers. Again, there's a temptation to focus on the leader as the key to winning over the rest. On the other hand, we may improve our odds by strengthening ties between each of the less resistant math teachers and advocates for the new approach in other departments.

If this tactic succeeds, we have gained two advantages. Followers tend to follow the nearest strong leader, so once they are won over, they tend to stay positive about the change. And one of the best ways to weaken a negative leader is to reduce the number of followers in that camp. A naysayer who feels increasingly alone is more likely to come over to the other camp in the end.

Teach and Model

We've all had students who just don't know how to apologize. When we insist, they fold their arms and mumble a surly "Sorry!" Other students express their emotions by rolling their eyes, glaring vindictively or lashing out. They just haven't been taught how to behave when they feel frustrated, sad, rejected, angry, or any combination of these. They're doing the best they can.

Now, you might be thinking that their parents should have taught them these important social skills. But for whatever reason, that hasn't happened. So you have options: You can put up with their behavior, you can complain, or you can teach and model appropriate behavior. Effective teachers choose the third option, which takes patience and persistence. Here's how Mr. Manners does it with his third graders. Starting with the whole class when the situation is calm, he role-plays a scenario, demonstrating the behavior that's acceptable in his classroom and in life. Some of the situations are positive; "please" and "thank you" go a long way. Other scenarios deal with negative situations, modeling how to defuse the tension or at least keep from escalating it. Teaching the whole class and then following up appropriately in individual cases helps his students develop the skills they need to succeed. Mr. Manners then makes a point of reinforcing the lesson with the whole class by praising the students when the classroom is humming along smoothly.

Effective leaders use the same approach when leading change in their schools: They teach and model the behaviors they expect, follow up with individuals in specific situations, and reinforce the lesson with the entire group. I call this the whole–part–whole approach.

An example I often use in school leadership presentations involves getting teachers to do their part in managing student behavior during all-school assemblies. We role-play a faculty meeting. As "principal," I ask the group, "Where do great teachers sit when they take their homeroom to an assembly?" The answer is always "With their students." My follow-up question is "Which students in particular?" They know that too: "The ones most likely to chitchat or act out."

Then I ask, "What about the less effective teachers?" Responses vary around a common theme: "They sit with other teachers, stand against the wall, stay in the back, don't even attend...." If they do sit with their students, they're not always paying attention to their behavior.

After a principal holds this five-minute conversation at a faculty meeting, everyone knows what teachers ought to be doing during assembly, and everyone knows that everyone else knows. Having made the expectation clear, the principal can talk with individuals who fall short about *how to meet it*, and fewer such conversations should be needed.

Finally, the principal can reinforce the behavior in remarks to the entire faculty: "Spirits were high at the Winter Carnival assembly, but thanks to the way you made your presence felt, the students were on their best behavior. I greatly appreciate the extra effort."

Practice Whole–Part–Whole

People often resist change simply because it involves doing something they haven't been taught to do. They're not comfortable getting into a situation that may call for skills they haven't mastered. To bring them around, you need to recognize this reluctance and deal with it up front. Again, you teach the entire group, follow up with individuals, and then reteach or reinforce the lesson with the entire group.

In the previous chapter, for example, we looked at the practice of videotaping classroom activity as a method for self-directed professional development. When school leaders introduce the program, teachers who have never experienced this process may hesitate to sign on. In our example, the roll-out begins with voluntary participation. When the time comes to integrate the practice school-wide, the whole–part–whole approach comes in handy.

At one staff meeting, you might take 10 minutes to role-play scenarios of videotaping classroom activity. In this case, you might start with a few situations that went laughably wrong. Perhaps the equipment malfunctioned and the teacher didn't find that out until too late. Perhaps the teacher privately reviewing the tape couldn't get past focusing on his appearance. Perhaps a peer feedback session fell flat because nobody came up with any comments at all. If you can get folks to laugh at these worst-case scenarios, they might feel more comfortable about venturing into new territory.

Then present a few examples of videotaping and review that went well. Perhaps a teacher learned that she was too quick to call on students after asking a question; now she gives them more time to think. Perhaps a peer review session ended up with science teachers adopting practices their colleague had used with good results in a lab experiment. Perhaps a video submitted with a grant application earned someone funding for a three-week geology field trip to Montana next summer!

Ten minutes should suffice to get the message across: This professional development activity is doable, and the expectation that every teacher will participate is reasonable. Does that mean you'll have full participation by next week? No, probably not. But you have made it clear to the entire group that you value and support this school-wide program. Now you can approach the holdouts individually to address any lingering concerns.

Step three is to reinforce participation on a group-wide basis. You can do this in a faculty meeting: "Just a quick shout-out to all of you who participated in video review sessions with your colleagues last week. This program is clearly improving our instruction." Or you can use your weekly *Friday Focus* bulletin (*Motivating and Inspiring Teachers*, Whitaker 2009): "Thanks to the camera crews who have videotaped 25 class sessions since September! Your efforts help make good teachers even better." This approach both encourages the folks who are participating and potentially tweaks the discomfort level of those who are not. School-wide, the program matures more quickly and its benefits become deep-rooted over the long term.

Keep Them Busy

Have you ever noticed the frequent overlap between the whiners and the slackers in an organization? The folks who do the least whine the most. The ones who are hard at work don't have the time or energy to gripe (although some still find time to cover for the laggards). When it comes to implementing change, leaders may also detect a certain amount of overlap between the whiner/slacker faction and the naysayers and foot-draggers. One tactic for reducing this resistance is to keep these negative individuals too busy to disrupt the positive forces for change.

You'll want to be selective about how you keep them occupied, of course. It would be counterproductive to put three of them on the committee working toward your school's reaccreditation. Every school has projects that take a certain amount of time and effort, are important but not essential, and have a public, visible, and positive outcome. A good example, in my experience, is the annual holiday party.

I love this mid-year morale booster, but it doesn't need the talents of a superstar. Instead, I looked to the other end of the effectiveness spectrum. Who needed to spend less time being negative and more time being productive? Before the first faculty meeting of the year, I individually asked three or four of these folks to join the holiday party planning committee. Since I was asking in August and they were not solely responsible, I could generally get them to sign on. They may also have seen this as a potential excuse for getting out of other duties. To counterbalance their well-known inclination to shirk the real work, I carefully avoided putting anyone on the committee who would be inclined to take up the slack.

At the opening faculty meeting, I introduced the holiday party planning committee, have them stand up for recognition, and invite other staff members to forward ideas and suggestions to one of them. To keep up the public pressure, I regularly wrote about them in my *Friday Focus* bulletin and had them present monthly reports at staff meetings. As long as they kept putting time and energy into the project, they got positive feedback from their colleagues—a good thing for them to experience. With work of their own to do, they were less inclined to gripe or obstruct the efforts of others.

If all went well in December, I congratulated them publicly and recruited them to plan the spring fling and the end-of-school picnic, knowing this would keep them busy for the rest of the year. If the party didn't go off without a hitch, at least it didn't really matter that much. I thanked them publicly, met with them privately to figure out what could have been planned differently—and *still* recruited them to put on the spring fling and the end-of-school picnic!

Control the Clusters

Naysayers, foot-draggers, whiners, and slackers can stand in the way of school improvement. When they cluster together, these obstacles form an imposing barrier. In presenting Strategy 2, *Make Sure the First Exposure Is Great!*, I discussed some tactics for dealing with this phenomenon during occasions such as staff meetings and site visits. I will now highlight additional opportunities to reduce the disruptive effect of negative clusters.

One occasion that comes to mind is a committee meeting or small-group discussion. These often take place around a rectangular table, with the committee chair or group leader typically sitting at one end. Experience indicates that the most negative or resistant group member tends to sit at the other end (directly opposite the leader) or even away from the table, against the wall (Figure 2A). To reduce this dynamic of resistance, the leader can choose another seat—not at one end of the table, but somewhere along the side. To further diminish the power of negativity, the leader or another positive person can deliberately arrive later and take a seat right beside the ringleader of resistance (Figure 2B).

Effective leaders continually watch for the development of negative clusters. Sometimes a particular event draws people together in opposition; sometimes they share similar beliefs. It may be that a particular person antagonizes several others without being aware of it, and a pocket of resistance forms.

Figure 2A

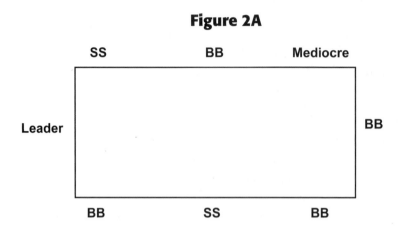

Figure 2B

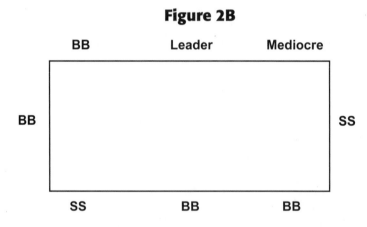

At other times, negative clusters may form out of convenience. If three teachers who tend to be negative just happen to have the same prep time, they may get in the habit of congregating for a regular afternoon gripe session. If they teach in the same department or at the same grade level, they may find common ground for ongoing complaints. Sometimes the triggering factor is proximity: their classrooms are on the same hall, or they carpool to work. Once it gets going, the griping feeds on itself.

In any of these instances, leaders can often take steps to respond. But with some thought and energy, they can also proactively discourage negative influences and encourage positive ones. They may not be able to manipulate schedules or room assignments, and they have no control over carpools, but they should notice when a new teacher is placed across the hall from a known negative force; perhaps a discreet heads-up or an extra check-in now and then is in order.

Count On the Disclosing (Alpha) Male

Groups and alliances can form for many reasons, some obvious and others not so obvious. People may connect because of their teaching assignments, age, or background. They may have children or grandchildren of about the same age; they may share a hobby or attend the same church. The list could go on and on. But to understand the dynamics of change in a school, we must address one particular group: the male cohort whose common ground lies in sports and coaching.

Many elementary schools have so few men on the staff that the testosterone factor is seldom relevant to decision making. Additionally, sports and coaching may not be much of a factor. However, in secondary schools we often find a faction of males (and some females) who may have a more tough-guy, macho approach to education.

In your particular setting, is there a cluster of men who go by "Coach" among their colleagues and students, past and present? Is there a table emotionally "reserved" for them, where most everyone knows the scores of the weekend's major league games, and most everyone would agree that team sports build character? If so, this message may be for you.

In itself, the presence of this group is neither good nor bad. It does not inherently merit appreciation or criticism. I'm a former coach myself, and I have no interest in debating the pros or cons of sports in schools or society. I simply acknowledge that in my experience, such a cohort of alpha male–dominated coaches may happen to collectively resist change when it comes to improving teaching and learning.

It's not that they constitute a negative cluster, but by and large, they feel very comfortable being in charge of what happens in their classrooms. They've mastered the ins and outs of a system that works for them, and in their world, game after game, season after season, the playing field and the rules stay the same.

Obviously, I am walking a fine line here, and in many schools this cohort does not even exist, but when this particular subset of resistance emerges, it requires a special solution. And because it's essential to bring along *all* the subgroups as you move forward with change and school improvement, you cannot afford to ignore this group.

The key to bringing them along is to have on board at least one "disclosing male" whom the others respect. What do I mean by "disclosing"? A disclosing person is willing to share and reflect publicly, either in a small-group setting or—far better for our purposes—in the presence of the whole staff. I'm not talking about someone who pontificates about the fine points of educational theory. As matter-of-factly as he discusses the varsity basketball team's performance on the foul line, the disclosing male might comment, "Yesterday when I was videotaping my class, I noticed that I tend to teach and address the left side of the room much more than the right side. Maybe it's because I'm right-handed, and that's the way I turn away from the board toward the class. I'm really going to work on balancing my instructional focus more evenly."

Coach (see there, I call him Coach, too) may or may not be the best teacher, although he works hard and is usually effective in the classroom. Self-aware and open to change, he would not hesitate to ask a colleague for help in framing higher-level thinking questions, for example. Another reason Coach is such a valuable asset when it comes to reducing resistance among this particular cohort is that he's an alpha male. The other coaches respect him.

Just as you develop tactics for getting Charlie Crabtree, Molly Moper, and Ben Blockitall to embrace change, you need to find ways to approach this crucial handful of people. If you don't have Coach on staff yet, you might look for him in your next round of hiring. He has the potential to bring a whole bunch of fence-sitters over to the side of the change you seek.

Strategy 6
Harness the Power of Emotion

| 1 | 2 | 3 | 4 | 5 | **6** | 7 | 8 | 9 |

"The research tells us…" is a common mantra in the field of education today. "Here's the data, so you must do this." Or conversely, "Show me the data or you can't do that." I take issue with this approach on a couple of counts.

First of all, research about what works or doesn't work in schools rarely involves a control group. We don't lock half of the third graders in a closet while we teach the other half, then bring them out and compare the results. The reality is much more complex than that. It is very difficult to isolate one variable or draw clear conclusions about cause and effect.

Second, if we think data alone will drive change, we're simply kidding ourselves. For one thing, we're dealing with people; no matter how hard we try, we can't simply mandate effective teaching. For another, the educational experience is very personal; there's no one best way to learn or to teach. Finally, we cannot ignore the power of emotion. Even hard-and-fast data won't convince people to change their ways if strong feelings are holding them back.

Diminish the Power of Fear

One of the biggest roadblocks to change is fear: fear of the unfamiliar, fear of failure, fear of embarrassment, and other fears we may not even recognize. Although they might not admit it, the main reason teachers resist having a colleague observe their classroom activities is the fear of being judged. It takes a lot of self-confidence to open that door.

Furthermore, we can't rely on logic to overcome this fear. Simply telling a resistant teacher that her colleague is a professional and therefore will refrain from judging her performance probably won't convince her to take the risk. Often, the only thing stronger than an emotion is another emotion.

Fear of Flying

You probably know someone who is afraid of flying—not specifically afraid of flying in the post–9/11 world, but just plain afraid of leaving the ground and going 30,000 feet up in the air confined in a metal cylinder. Anyone who's ever sat in an airplane next to a nervous fellow passenger gripping the arms of her seat knows that this dread is very real.

You might try to soothe your seatmate by talking about how well pilots are trained or how safely planes are engineered nowadays. You probably won't mention that yes, planes do crash, and conceivably this one could, but you might comment that statistically, plane travel is safer than driving or even than walking around a major city. Because you're not afraid of flying, these facts and statistics make a lot of sense to you. Your arguments are so logical, so rational. Why is she still gripping the arms of her seat?

If you ask her that question, she'll readily admit that her dread of flying is rooted in emotion, not in logic, and that she's been afraid of flying all her life. She doesn't have a reason—she's never experienced an emergency landing or known anyone who's been in a crash. Your facts and statistics don't change the way she feels, but think about it: She's on this plane, even though she's afraid of flying. What force had the power to overcome that fear? Well, why not ask her *that*?

Flying Anyway

It turns out that her only daughter, who lives in Boston, has just given birth to her third grandchild, and she had promised to help out with the other kids for a few weeks. She usually travels by train—the Southwest Chief from Santa Fe to Chicago, then the Lake Shore Limited—but it takes a couple of days, and the baby came three weeks early, and her husband found a seat on a direct flight and drove her right to the airport. She hardly had time to pack!

She shows you pictures of the older children; Johnny is seven, Katie is three. Don't they look like peas in a pod? She can't wait to meet Sarah, who's not even one day old. She tells you funny stories about when Johnny and Katie were babies. By now, guess what: Grandma isn't gripping the arms of her seat anymore. She's so relaxed, it startles her to hear the copilot announce that it's time to return our tray tables and seat backs to their original upright and locked position!

It took the strong pull of motherhood to overcome her dread of flying and get her on that plane. In the workplace, leaders can counteract the fear of change by harnessing the power of similar connections.

Make It Seem As If Everyone Is Doing It

The need to belong is a very strong motivator. One way to get everyone—superstars, backbones, and mediocres—on the bandwagon for change is to make it seem as if most of their colleagues are already on board. You started with the superstars, the new teachers, and other points of least resistance. Once you've achieved a critical mass of participation, it's time to go after the holdouts.

Here, the isolated situation of the classroom teacher can work to your advantage, especially if the change you seek is a matter of individual practice, such as having teachers videotape their classroom activities for self-directed professional development. In discussing Strategy 4, *Find the Entry Points*, we suggested launching that program through individual sign-ups with the media center specialist rather than asking teachers to indicate interest by a public show of hands. Those who opt to participate know who they are. As they grow more comfortable with the practice, some might share comments about their experiences with colleagues in private. Some will feel fine about offering examples of its benefits at a faculty meeting, as we described in exploring Strategy 5, *Reduce the Resistance.* The holdouts really don't know how many others are in the same boat. They may wonder, "Am I the only one *not* doing this?" That emotional pressure to be part of the group may overcome their fear of being judged.

Make the New Seem Normal

We can take steps to reinforce the impression that almost everyone has signed on to this program. The principal—let's call her Mrs. Proactive—can set a good example by asking a colleague to videotape a faculty meeting, then writing about it in her next *Friday Focus:* "Now I see why so many of you say how valuable you have found this practice. After reviewing the way I managed Wednesday's faculty meeting, I realized that there are several things I might do differently...." The specific ideas drawn from the self-reflection don't matter here as much as the indication that *"so many of you"* have found the practice valuable.

Or she might write, "Several of you had expressed concern about how quickly you have been going through DVDs, CDs, or videotapes as you record your classes. No worries. A new supply has just arrived, so we are stocked up through the holidays. Have at it, gang!"

This lets the individuals who have chosen to participate know that they're not alone. Furthermore, it sends the reassuring message that people who have tried the practice come back for more, which may encourage those who haven't signed on to give it a try.

Again, we do this after we have reached a critical mass of participation. We don't want to make videotaping classroom activities seem special, something only the superstars will do. Many people don't think of themselves as special, and they may shy away from the program if they think they're going to be singled out and put in the spotlight.

Rather, we want to make this seem normal, just part of the routine, as we do when interviewing potential new hires.

Privately, of course, you can, and should, thank every individual who is taking the lead in getting the program underway. You can ask whether they would be willing to participate in role-playing scenarios at a faculty meeting, as described in the last chapter. Pulling together a group to do this may be easier and more effective than singling out just one or two. Try to get participants from across the spectrum of teachers—Mr. Oscar, who loves the spotlight; Mrs. Malarkey, who used this as a way to improve her classroom management skills; Ms. Rookie, who can talk about how the program was part of what drew her to this school; and if you can get Coach to talk about how this makes so much sense to him because he does it all the time with his team, letting them watch their performance and developing tips for improving their techniques, you may be amazed at the impact.

Make Everyone Want In

The same approach works when you ask for full participation right from the start. At one school where I was principal, I had developed the habit of calling parents with positive feedback and follow-up calls about their children's satisfactory performance and behavior on a regular basis. After a time, our teacher leadership team decided that this approach to school improvement would be even more powerful if the positive phone calls also came from teachers.

When we first discussed the idea, there was concern that some teachers would probably not make the phone calls. My response was, "Let's not let the ones who won't do it stand in the way of those who will. Sure, we want full participation, but aren't we better off if even one teacher adopts the practice? We can't get to 100 percent participation if we don't start at all, and we're more likely to get there if we set that expectation right from the beginning." So the leadership team presented the plan to the faculty: Every week, every teacher would make one positive phone call to a parent of his or her choosing.

The "Dial It Up" program got off to a strong start. A handful of teachers who had been doing this for years just kept doing it. Some who already felt comfortable communicating with parents found that it was particularly rewarding to call with good news! Others gave it a try and also experienced this reinforcement. Because teachers could choose which parent to call, they set themselves up for a positive first exposure by starting with the ones most likely to express appreciation. As they continued the practice, some even made more than one call a week.

The next step was to create an environment in which the ones who weren't participating felt left out. I started by compiling a list of teachers I knew were "frequent phoners" and asking them how it was going. If they reported good experiences, as they nearly always did, I'd ask if they'd be willing to share their stories at an upcoming staff meeting. When I had several volunteers lined up, I made my move.

Toward the end of one meeting, I started to wrap it up, and then I casually inquired, "By the way, have any of you had a chance to make those Dial It Up calls?" As I expected, many raised their hands. I called on the "safe" ones, the ones whose feedback I had previewed. One by one, they described how easy it was, how well it went, how much they enjoyed the experience. After thanking them, I relayed some of the appreciative comments I'd heard from many parents, although I didn't identify the parents by name. I ended the meeting by congratulating the entire staff for their commitment to Dial It Up.

I'll have more to say about reinforcing actions through public praise when we come to Strategy 8, *Reinforce Changed Behaviors*. For now, let's focus on the effect. Those who had made Dial It Up calls felt appreciated, whether they'd had a chance to describe their experiences in the meeting or not, and those who hadn't made calls were more likely to want in on the fun.

Over the next month or so, I added to the pressure (in a nonthreatening way) by continuing to ask individuals how

Dial It Up was going for them. If they indicated that they hadn't started yet, I'd simply say I was looking forward to hearing about it when they had the chance. Each time I did this, the very fact that I asked was enough to strengthen the impression that this was an established practice at our school. In a relatively short time, the environment was such that a teacher who hadn't made Dial It Up a habit felt like the odd man out.

Give Two Incentives for Change

It's eight o'clock on a Thursday morning at Riverdale Middle School. As usual, the day begins with the principal's "remarks and announcements" over the intercom. Apologizing for the late notice, she tells everyone that this afternoon at two, a special all-school assembly will replace the classes ordinarily held in that block.

In Room 6, Ms. Marvel throws up her hands in dismay. She had planned for one of her Language Arts sections to present poetry projects that afternoon, and now that can't happen. She knows that the students will be disappointed. Some of them had even brought in costumes and memorized poems! Ms. Marvel hates to let them down at the last minute like this.

Across the hall, Mr. Middling is also annoyed; he ordinarily has planning time in the last block (and sometimes he manages to turn it into free time). Next door, Ms. Mediocre mutters under her breath. She teaches five sections of history each day, and the assembly will put her last-period section one day behind the rest. Now she'll have to find a DVD to show the other four sections so she can get them all back on the same schedule. (It's just not fair to expect her to keep track when they get out of sync!)

Now, how do these teachers react when they have two weeks' advance notice about a scheduling switch like this one?

Ms. Marvel thinks to herself, "I wonder if there is anything I should do to prepare my students?" Or she asks the principal, "Should I be planning follow-up discussions and activities?" Across the hall, Mr. Middling is annoyed, because the assembly interferes with his planning time. And next door, Ms. Mediocre starts looking for a DVD so she can keep all her sections doing the same thing on the same day.

Finally, how would these teachers react to a proposed or mandated change in the way things are done in their school or district? As you've probably figured out by now, Ms. Marvel would look at its impact on instruction and learning. If we show her that doing things differently is best for students, she will support the change—even if it means more work for her.

Mr. Middling and Ms. Mediocre take a very different view. First and foremost, they look out for their own interests. They definitely do everything they can to avoid more work. If we want them to support change, we must convince them that doing things differently is best *for them.*

This means that when we want *all* the educators in our school or district to support the change we seek, we must offer two incentives right from the start. Of course, we will make every effort to show that doing things differently is *best for our students.* But to draw support from across the spectrum, we must also show teachers how doing things differently is *best for them.*

The majority of teachers are positive and productive. They chose education to make a difference in the lives of young people, and they bring their hearts as well as their minds to their work. Giving them reasons that something is good for the students is the emotional tug they need to buy in, but if we truly do want everyone on board, we have to be up front about the more selfish reasons to participate. Although this may seem like a criticism, it really comes down to facing the reality about moving an entire group forward.

The Emotions of the First Exposure

To maximize the odds of a positive initial response, you must channel the emotions triggered by the first exposure to an impending change. One way is to highlight the good outcomes that will result from this change. When my teacher leadership team launched the Dial It Up program, for example, they emphasized that parents said good things to the principal about the teachers who were already making such calls.

Another way to increase your chances of a good reaction is to highlight the negatives that the change will diminish or forestall, such as the confrontational attitude some parents bring to conferences. "The Dial It Up program will get parents on our side!"

Likewise, if we want to encourage all the teachers in our building to be in the hallways as students move between classes, we might tell an emotional story of how two strapping senior boys were on the brink of harassing a timid freshman when a teacher stepped out of her classroom: When the boys saw her, they just kept walking down the hallway instead. Then we could emphasize that the "hallway habit" makes our school a safer place for all of our students (incentive #1), and it makes our school a better place for all of us (incentive #2).

Often, the personal incentive that convinces Mr. Middling or Ms. Mediocre to get with the program can be something as simple as seeking praise or avoiding embarrassment. That's one very good reason to set the expectation of 100 percent participation right from the beginning. Then it's perfectly natural for the leader to ask, "Hey, how's it going with Dial It Up?" Teachers who have to admit that they haven't made a call yet will feel uncomfortable, and soon they'll start to think that the best thing *for them* just might be to pick up the phone!

The Logic of Logic

We shouldn't discount the power of a rational and systematic approach. (After all, we need the math teachers on board too!) Of course, any hard data, statistical indications, literature reviews, and even anecdotal evidence will help convince professional educators about the benefits of change, but we can't lead change with logic alone. Given the diversity of skill sets, perspectives, and backgrounds within any organization, logic tells us that we need a two-fold approach: We need to win both minds *and* hearts.

Embarking on change can be a lot like setting out on a journey. If you know where you are headed and have a strong incentive to go there, it's a lot easier to pack your bags and get going. If you want all of your staff members to travel with you, you need to get them onto that airplane. This means finding an incentive powerful enough to overcome any worries or fears they may have. Once you make the commitment and take off, you're on your way. Ready? Buckled in? Let's do it!

Strategy 7
Look Past Buy-In to Action

| 1 | 2 | 3 | 4 | 5 | 6 | **7** | 8 | 9 |

I'd love to have 100 percent agreement on any change before I implement it. How could my efforts go wrong? But if I waited for 100 percent agreement, I'd never get around to implementing change at all. As they say in poker, "If you think too long, you may think wrong." Practically speaking, I can think of many situations I don't want to be thinking too long and hard about. It would be neat if all five members of my family agreed on what restaurant to go to before we got in the car, but we do need to get going before the restaurant closes! At some point, enough is enough.

A couple of days ago, I gave a presentation to a group of educators I hold in high regard. After lunch, a few of them commented that they had been discussing my books and comparing them with books written by another author. Weighing the pros and cons of each, they concluded that the other author "made them think about education differently." I felt a twinge of envy; that's quite a compliment. But they went on to say, "Your books make us *act* differently." To me, that's even better.

I believe their reflections have a direct connection with the change we hope to achieve, and need to achieve, in our schools. It's good for people to think differently about education, but what really matters is for them to act differently. I'd love it if every teacher thought hard about treating students with respect, but as nice as that would be, what I really want is for them to actually treat every single student with respect, every single day.

What a joy teaching would be if every teacher liked every student, but as my dad used to say, "If wishes were horses, beggars would ride." We can't afford to let the ideal goal keep us from reaching a realistic objective, any more than we can afford to wait around until the ideal conditions for change present themselves. Maybe that focus on the ideal is what leads others to say that it takes three to eight years to achieve significant change. What if we focus on something a little more concrete? What if we tell our teachers, "Whether you like a student or not, *act* as if you do"? Isn't this a more reasonable, achievable, and even measurable goal? You bet it is!

The Tennessee Tornado

I've always been afraid of heights, so it's not surprising that I also hated roller coasters. For years and years, my wife was the designated roller-coaster sidekick for our oldest daughter, who thinks they're a blast—especially the one at the county fair called the Tennessee Tornado.

Well, one year my wife was pregnant when county fair days rolled around, so the Tennessee Tornado was off limits. My little girl turned pleadingly to me. Not wanting to disappoint her, Daddy toughed it out. And you know what? For the part when I actually had my eyes open, it wasn't that bad. As a matter of fact, I kind of liked it. I wasn't thrilled that she wanted to go again and again, but gradually it became easier for me. Now the two of us ride all the roller coasters together, and we both really enjoy them.

My son takes after me in the fear department. I'm afraid of heights; he's afraid of heights. I'm afraid of snakes; he's afraid of snakes. I'm afraid of his mother; he's ... (just kidding on that one, dear). He never had any interest at all in the Tennessee Tornado, but he's fascinated by the heavens, astronauts, and outer space, so one year an indoor ride called Space Mountain caught his eye. Little did he know it was a roller coaster! Of course, he almost freaked out at the first terrifying downhill rush, but by the time the ride was over, he was grinning with delight. Now he's as much a fan of thrill rides as anyone in our family.

Taking Stock of the Exchange

We have referred many times to the idea of having teachers exchange visits to observe in each other's classrooms. We described starting the program with superstars and new hires—the points of least resistance—to maximize the odds that the first exposure will be positive. We recommend this approach because teachers who have a good experience the first time will be more comfortable repeating it and will soon start to see its benefits. Having experienced it themselves they are then less likely to be swayed by a colleague who might scoff that exchanging classroom visits is just a waste of time and effort.

If you've never been on a roller coaster and your dad says he hates that kind of ride, you will probably be leery of them. Even after your dad tries it and becomes a fan, you might hang back, but if for some reason you end up riding Space Mountain, you might see things differently. You just might want to try it again, and even if your mom advises you that the bigger roller coasters are scarier, you might give the Tennessee Tornado a whirl! You'd be willing to find out for yourself.

A School Is Not the County Fair

Sometimes people need to experience a situation firsthand before they come around to thinking it's a good idea. When it comes to leading change, at some point you may need to say, "You don't have to buy into the idea, but because you're a professional working in this school, I expect you to give it a try. Now, how would you like to start?"

School leadership is more complicated than taking the kids to the county fair. For one thing, you should think twice before deciding that 100 percent participation is truly essential. It might be nice to have every single teacher out in the hallway between classes, but it might be even nicer if a couple of the negative force staff members stay in their rooms. As long as the teachers with the "hallway habit" feel valued for their contribution to improving the school climate, they are not likely to care one bit if a handful of others don't do their part. If they don't feel valued, they'll resent being expected to do hallway duty whether everyone is out there or not.

On the other hand, when you do decide that full participation is in order, you will want to get as many supporters as possible on board before you make that big move. Every teacher who is already participating at that point is one fewer teacher who will feel "forced" to participate and therefore inclined to resist. One of Yogi Berra's famous malapropisms became the title of his third book: *When You Come to a Fork in the Road, Take It*. How do you get to that fork in the road? How do you map your progress along the way?

Time to Get Graphic

Deciding to embark on change can be daunting, particularly when you anticipate expecting full participation. Even in a school building with only 20 staff members, the thought of trying to get all of them to support your effort may make you reluctant to even try. To make the task more manageable, you need to get graphic. The model described on the next few pages will help you take charge of change.

The objective is to lay out a visual representation of the people in your organization, identifying the key entry points and where they lead. As you will notice, this builds on Strategy 3: *Determine Who Matters Most*.

Using a computer, a SMARTboard, chalkboard, or whiteboard, or simply a large sheet of blank paper, start at the top of the page. List the superstars in your organization who are most likely to support the change you plan to implement. (Figure 3 shows an example.)

Next, draw links connecting each of these key individuals with each of the people they will most likely be able

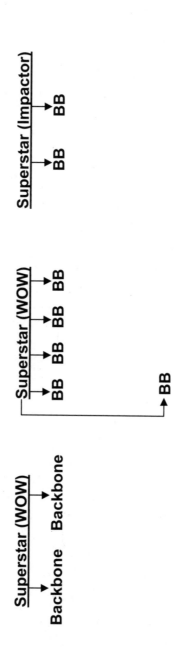

Figure 3

to influence. Then identify any strong connections between the people in this second tier and the people they can bring along. At the same time, start new stems with the backbone staff members that are likely to play key roles in implementing your plan. Keep in mind that this may include new hires who have already agreed to take part. Once again, draw links from these individuals to others that they may help bring along (Figure 4).

You can and should repeat this mapping at several points along the way. After a while, a familiar pattern may emerge, because the superstars play so many roles within any organization.

Creating this visual web may dramatically simplify what was once an overwhelming task. You no longer have to think about convincing all 20 staff members, or all 60, or all 120. Instead, you can focus on the four or eight key players. How will you approach them to win their backing? How will you support their efforts to influence others?

In the instance just described, the process of mapping entry points and links depended on your knowledge and understanding of the *informal dynamics* among your staff. You can also think about the *formal organization* of a school as you identify key points of least resistance. Whether it's an elementary school with multiple teachers at a grade level, a middle school with interdisciplinary teams, or a high school with departments by subject area, can you single out people who would be likely to support your plan and can positively influence a certain group? This might be a formal leader, such as the math department chair. However, it might just as easily be an informal player who operates from the middle of the pack on the sixth-grade team. Either way, write their names down and draw the links to the second tier of individuals they influence, then the third.

Scaling It Up or Down

District-level leaders can follow the same approach to map the links for promoting change throughout the dis-

Figure 4

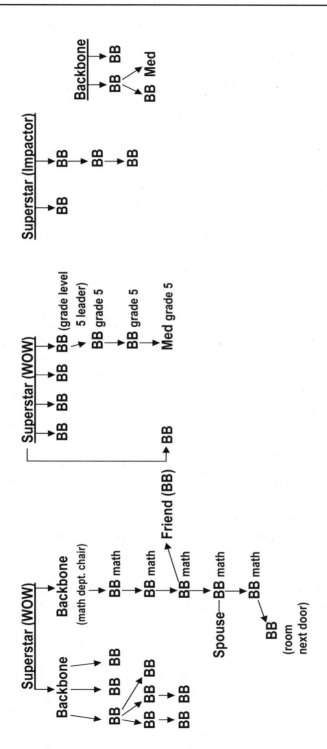

trict, whether that means two schools or two hundred. Which superstar principals can manage change effectively in their own buildings because they have strong support from the vast majority of their faculty and staff? Write down their names and map the links. Can they also influence their fellow principals? Map those links as well. Does the district special education director have a good working relationship with most of the special education teachers? Write that name down too, and map the links. Don't forget the third-tier links: Which classroom teachers can the individual special ed teachers help bring on board? Figures 5 and 6 illustrate this mapping.

The process works equally well for planning and tracking changes on a smaller scale, such as within a department or at a particular grade level. Think about the points of least resistance; identify the positive influences. Write down these names and map the links. In my experience, the most challenging situation for implementing change occurs when we hope to move a relatively small group that does not have a superstar, an outstanding role model, or a strong positive personality. In that case, it becomes crucial to create a direct link or links to outside support. This might be another group within the school, a building- level leader, or someone from a different educational center.

At all levels, the superstars constitute critical entry points for two reasons: They have the greatest positive influence on others, and they have the broadest vision. Their view of a proposed change takes into consideration its effect on the whole setting. They will tell us what they think: Is it a good idea? Are there ways to make it even better? What is the best approach to implementing it? Who should be involved in the process, and at what stage?

Depending on the size of the group and the breadth of the change, you may need to bring in some (or many) backbones as well. Perhaps we will need to work directly with certain mediocres who could put up roadblocks if not consulted in advance. We probably can't manage change effectively using *only* our superstars, but we have very little chance of doing so without them.

Figure 5

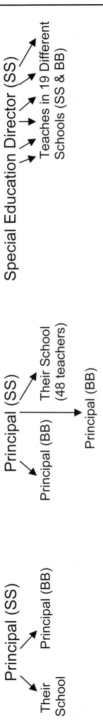

Figure 6

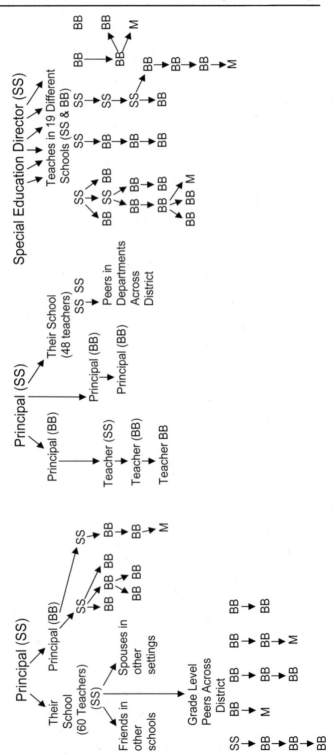

The Balance Shifts

So, starting with the superstars, you set out along the road you have mapped out. Gradually, more and more people implement and/or accept the change. Keep in mind that for some, acceptance happens first, but many others have to experience the new way in action before they can start to see its benefits. Little by little, the balance shifts. You can almost color-code your map, shading in the links to track the progress of change as it moves from the entry points to the second tier and then the third. As time goes on, the unshaded portion—the people who have neither implemented nor accepted the change—becomes the minority. The old culture fades out as a new culture takes root.

Imposing the change across the board at this point will affect many fewer people (Figure 7). Because of the way you planned your approach, the holdouts are likely to be folks who folks who generally balk at improvement efforts of any type. By now they probably don't have much support in their resistance, and the more it seems that everyone else is on board, the more likely it becomes that the foot-draggers will follow along. Nobody's really paying any attention to their carping, and there's nobody interesting left in their club!

Look Out the Windshield,
Not the Rearview Mirror

One other impediment to change is the past. Many people, and especially those who tend to resist change, love to live in the past. Thinking of the good old days gives them great comfort. Furthermore, looking back gives them a plateful of excuses: "We did this nine years ago, and it didn't work," or "The last principal we had kept changing the system every year, and nobody ever knew what was going on," or "We worked really hard to develop these procedures. Why tinker with something that's not broken?"

Now, their memories may or may not be accurate, and their objections may or may not be legitimate, but as lead-

Figure 7

Initiating the Change Process

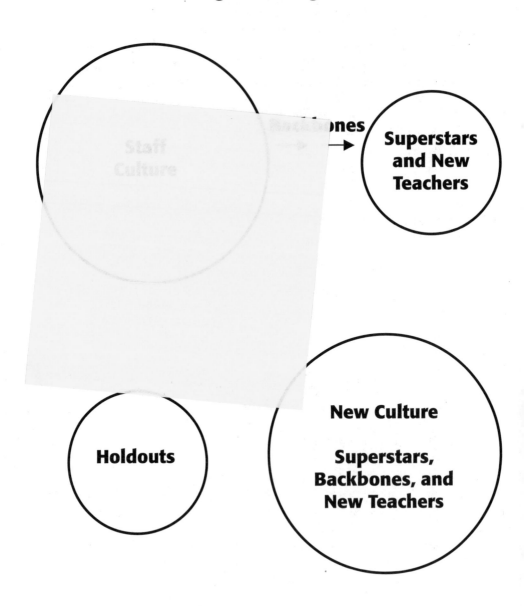

Backbones → Superstars and New Teachers

Staff Culture

Holdouts

New Culture

Superstars, Backbones, and New Teachers

ers, we have to make sure their fondness for days gone by doesn't keep us from moving forward. We may never know exactly what past events or decisions brought our organization to where it is today. It's quite likely there were great reasons for implementing certain practices that now seem outdated. It's entirely possible that mistakes were made; after all, nobody's perfect, and no organization does everything right 100 percent of the time. All we can do is to learn from past mistakes and do our best not to repeat them. We don't have to criticize the current situation. We can acknowledge the efforts of the people who worked to get to this point and honor the past without being stuck in it. We must consistently look to the future. A useful question for school leaders in any situation that involves change is this: "As good as we are, how can we be even better?"

If you want to steer your organization down the road to change, you have to keep looking forward, through the windshield. By the time opportunities appear in the rearview mirror, it's too late to take advantage of them. And if obstacles lie ahead, you certainly want to do whatever you can to avoid them. Regardless of what happened in the past, everyone wants the future to be better.

So When Do We Pull the Trigger?

There is no foolproof way to know exactly when to sound that starting gun and implement your plan across the board. Every situation is different, and every group of people has its own idiosyncrasies. If you move too quickly to force change, too many folks will set their minds against it and never come around. If you wait too long, the momentum can fade away.

If you're asking all of your staff to commit to a new procedure or structure that's relatively simple and requires no additional work on their part, you can probably just say the word without too much advance preparation. As a general rule, however, the best time to issue a mandate for change is after the balance has shifted in its favor. Make your best effort to get all the superstars on board; give those key

players time to work their magic on as many of their colleagues as possible. Then watch for the critical mass to
emerge. Take advantage of the start of a new school year,
when everybody is on their best behavior, and go for it.
Strategy 8 provides insight on what to do after you take
that fork in the road.

Strategy 8

Reinforce Changed Behaviors

| 1 | 2 | 3 | 4 | 5 | 6 | 7 | **8** | 9 |

everyday practice. Such efforts yield much more authentic professional growth than can be gained from outsiders presenting to the faculty in an "ongoing" program that hits the Pause button the minute they turn off the microphone and doesn't resume until they return a month later.

Conversely, if the school's or district's leaders do not discuss, facilitate opportunities for, and show interest in a new concept, it will most likely fade into oblivion regardless of the buzz generated in a dynamic presentation, workshop, or conference. Even if—against all odds—a handful of teachers who attended an off-site workshop continue to explore and implement the ideas introduced there, without the support and encouragement of the school's leadership, the benefits will likely not extend beyond those few. There is no question that the new will never become the normal without an ongoing effort to integrate change into the everyday routine of a school. Fortunately, in the long run effective leadership matters more than money, and it's a variable you can control.

Reinforce at Every Step

Change can be a difficult and occasionally painful process. Even in a perfect world, it moves forward in fits and starts. In all organizations, the journey toward change arouses various levels of interest among those being encouraged to travel that road. Some manage only baby steps; others take two steps forward and then one step back. Because of this erratic progress, leaders must reinforce these efforts at every point along the way.

Say you'd like to improve the attendance habits of the students in your school. One tradition is to honor those with perfect attendance at an assembly as the school year draws to a close. That's a nice gesture, but unfortunately few students manage to maintain perfect attendance, and it might not be perceived as "cool" to be the only kid who never missed a day of seventh grade. Some schools post attendance numbers daily as a way to emphasize the need to show up at school every day. There are no downsides to this, except that the daily tally can tend to fade into background noise and lose its effect.

On their own, some teachers make a personal attempt to reinforce student attendance. Ms. Marvel announces with a big smile, "Class, this is the seventh day in a row that everyone has been here. It sure is exciting to see each of you today! I'm so lucky to get to work with you." Follow-up comments could include sharing that the record for attendance in her classroom is 16 consecutive days with everyone there; wouldn't it be fun to see if this class can eclipse that mark? This type of emotional feedback is a very valuable component of positively reinforcing behaviors.

Which sort of feedback is more likely to keep you on a diet—"You're looking great!" or "It's about time"? And when do you want to hear encouraging compliments about your weight loss—after you've shed 35 pounds, or when you're still getting used to the taste of *Slim·Fast*? Spaced reinforcement (early and often) can go a lot farther than massed reinforcement in supporting a regular effort to improve habits in the classroom.

Out from Behind the Desk

Let's imagine that one change the school leadership team would like to bring about is to have teachers spend less time sitting behind their desks and more time up and about, interacting with students. In many schools, this could make a big difference in improving the teaching and learning that goes on during class time. How might we encourage teachers to make this a habit? One possibility is to have a guest speaker address effective instructional practices in a dynamic and memorable presentation. Teachers could also attend professional development sessions and come back fired up about the benefits of an interactive approach to teaching. Think about it, though: Isn't it likely that teachers already know they should get out from behind their desks? They're just not doing it.

You may have your suspicions about why they don't spend more time up and about in their classrooms. Maybe they simply run out of energy; maybe they lack confidence in their ability to interact effectively; maybe they're not even aware of how often they sit behind the desk. Whatever the cause, you probably would like to increase the physical interaction between teachers and students in many of your classrooms. Is there a way to boost this behavior without outside intervention or resources?

Well, Mrs. Proactive might take up the topic in her *Friday Focus* staff memo, or even at a faculty meeting:

> The other day, chatting with a few of our outstanding teachers, I asked them this question: "Can you tell me when you sit behind your desk during class time?"
>
> I expected answers along the lines of "hardly ever," or even "never," because in my mental image of effective teachers, they're up and about, interacting with students. Their answers were more sophisticated than that. As I expected, when they're doing *instructor-driven teaching* they're on the move. They also said that the vast majority of the time when students are doing individual seat work, they continue to walk around the room, looking over shoulders, answering questions, and paying attention to behavior during this *guided practice* phase.
>
> What I found really interesting was that on some occasions, they really want students to work independently, completely on their own, and they've learned that if they continue to walk around the room, the students will ask for help, because normally that's what the teacher is there for. If they're standing right there, it sounds off-putting to say "I need you to do this on your own." So during this *independent practice* time, they remove themselves, emotionally and physically, by sitting behind their desks.
>
> Now of course, students might still raise their hands with a question, or even come up and ask for guidance, but the teachers feel much more comfortable saying "I'm sorry, but this time you really need to try to do it on your own."

After sharing the perspectives of these teachers, Mrs. Proactive could then add a personal commentary:

> Wow! I'm continually impressed with the sophisticated thinking and attention to detail that you bring to your work. Over the next month or so, I'm going to make a special effort to ask each of you about when you choose to sit behind your desk. From what these teachers say, your choices really do make a difference!

Now if Mrs. Proactive pops into classrooms on a regular basis, and if her *Friday Focus* message hits its mark, it's very likely that on Monday morning fewer teachers will be taking it easy behind their desks. Now Mrs. Proactive has a chance to write a brief note to everybody she sees up and about in the classroom over the next few weeks, thanking them for putting in the time and energy to be so engaged with their students.

Keep in mind that the only way this in-house professional development will be ongoing rather than a one-shot deal is if "up and about" continues to be part of the dialogue in the school. At a staff meeting several weeks later—or, better yet, in the *Friday Focus*—Mrs. Proactive might share something along these lines:

> During the past few days, I dropped in on a number of classrooms, and in almost every one of them you were up and about, interacting with students, monitoring seat work, and paying attention to good classroom behavior. I say "almost every one" because in Ms. Marvel's class, the students were working independently on memorizing poems for the Poetry Jam next week, and Ms. Marvel was at her desk putting the finishing touches on the program. I would describe the atmosphere in that classroom as a quiet buzz!
>
> I appreciate all of your energy and effort, and so do our students! We are so lucky to have you in this school. I don't know how you do it at this time of the year, but it sure does make a difference. Thanks for being such great professionals, and I'll see you at the Poetry Jam!"

This accomplishes several objectives we have discussed. First, it involves some emotional reinforcement, which can be more effective and meaningful than dry logic. Second, it keeps the dialogue in the open, rather than simply bringing the topic to the teachers' attention once and then letting it drift off the radar screen. Third, it gives the strong impression that practically everyone is following the practice Mrs. Proactive has highlighted. This approach teaches people the right way to do things, reinforces those who do things that way, and potentially discomfits those who haven't yet adopted the practices you want to encourage.

Public versus Private Praise

One of the tricky decisions for a leader is whether to use public or private praise to reinforce the positive. If in doubt, it is always safe to use private reinforcement. Yet, public praise can be a useful way to encourage the spread of the behavior youchoose to highlight. The downside is the risk that praising individuals in public can put them in the spotlight in a way that's uncomfortable for them, annoying to their peers, and potentially unhelpful in reinforcing the positive.

Two key questions can help you decide when public praise is appropriate and useful. The first question is, "Are we trying to *recognize a person,* or are we trying to *reinforce an action?*" If Savanna writes an outstanding poem for the Poetry Jam, Ms. Marvel should recognize her achievement; if Marcos struggles for an hour and comes up with four simple lines that rhyme, Ms. Marvel should applaud his effort. But it might be more appropriate to make these comments in private. Singling out a student for public recognition can generate resentment among the rest of the class, especially if it happens over and over again.

When the goal is to reinforce an action, public praise can be a powerful tool. If the kindergarteners come in from the playground and settle down for the Weekly Weather Watch, telling them "Thank you so much for getting quiet right away! You even remembered to hang up your coats.

Good job!" is a way to teach and reinforce the right habits for the transition from outside play to indoor learning. If three teachers come in on a Saturday to transform the drab, disorganized resource center they share into an attractive space that improves student learning, I'll sure want to highlight that in the next *Friday Focus*. It just might motivate others to do the same!

This brings us to the second question about public versus private praise: "Are we trying to reinforce an action *that everyone can do*?" Not everyone can earn a 3.5 GPA; think twice about recognizing these high achievers publicly in your setting. When Mrs. Proactive wanted to get more teachers out from behind their desks—reinforcing a practice that was within every teacher's ability—she was careful not to name the first three "outstanding teachers" she quoted. That might have shifted the focus from the practice to the people she named, and singling out the superstars can generate resentment among their colleagues.

Instead, Mrs. Proactive chose to use *anonymous* public praise. "During the past few days, I dropped in on a number of classrooms, and in almost every one of them you were up and about. ... I appreciate all of your energy and effort, and so do our students! It sure does make a difference." The teachers who had practiced interactive teaching assumed the praise was meant for them, and everyone got the message that the practice is valued at this school.

Reinforce the Attempts Too

Everyone loves a winner—just check the attendance figures at any sports venue. If the home team is on a winning streak or headed for the playoffs, it's tough to get a ticket. During a losing season, though, sports fans may be selling their seats for a game or two, or even trying to give their tickets away.

The scoreboard for change in your school may not be quite as clear-cut as the ones at the baseball stadium. It's not always obvious whether the team is winning or losing, whether the players are sharpening their skills or heading into a slump, or even whether it's the fifth inning or the ninth. That can make the process of implementing change a frustrating experience for the leaders and perhaps for the entire staff. And anytime we take risks, we are going to have both successes and failures.

However, the odds of success increase if you remember to cheer the team on, and not just when you chalk up a win. Change happens incrementally, so we need to applaud the baby steps in the right direction. Growth takes place in unexpected spurts, so you need to acknowledge efforts even if they fall a little flat. Just because something didn't work out as well as you hoped doesn't mean the attempt was not worthwhile. This may be particularly true with some of your more reluctant risk takers. Simply trying their hand at a new approach may be more of a challenge for them than striving for success is for a superstar. They're more likely to keep trying if you consistently reinforce their attempts.

Set Up for Success

The very best teachers make every student feel valued. They know who may struggle with a math problem; they know who may be reluctant to speak up in English class. They also keep close tabs on student seat work, so they know when these students are on the right track, and that's when they ask them to participate more publicly. They set them up for success, reinforce their attempts, and build on them. Little by little, they draw them into a wider range of experiences that may involve more and more risk taking. Each positive reinforcement paves the way for additional opportunities and experiences in the future.

Likewise, the very best leaders value every person on their staff and make every effort to nurture their professional growth. Under Strategy 5, *Reduce the Resistance*, we described keeping the negative forces too busy to obstruct change by asking them to take responsibility for the holiday party—and then the spring fling and the end-of-school picnic. Consistently reinforcing their positive contributions to a project of that scope and importance might make them more inclined to work well with a couple of backbones on another committee where the outcome matters more. If *that* experience goes well, you can look for an opportunity to include them in a project that might lure them out of their comfortable rut. Little by little, they might become more willing to take risks. Remember, hiring better people is just one half of the equation for improving your school. It's equally important to improve the people you've got!

As always, you'll want to keep tabs on the situation. If it turns out that the other committee members are putting in a disproportionate amount of work and energy, make sure to express your appreciation privately to them. If they know that you know, they are much more likely to accept the challenge and less likely to resent sharing the public praise with someone who has contributed less.

Don't Miss That Moment

As leaders, we must remember that sometimes the most significant change starts with an inconspicuous shift in direction. The very best leaders keep close tabs on the staff members who aren't eager to change their ways, watching for a step in the right direction and reinforcing that behavior. They don't necessarily make a big deal of it in public, but they do express their appreciation, either in person or with a brief note: "Wow, what a traffic jam in the hallways this morning! Everybody was in a hurry because two of the buses were running late, and it made a difference to have you at that busy intersection outside your classroom. Thanks! I look forward to seeing you there again tomorrow."

If Mr. Middling has resisted making Dial It Up calls, the principal might spend some time in his classroom and watch for an opening. "Say, didn't Joon Won do a good job explaining that algebra problem? His mom would be so proud. You've met her at the soccer games, right? She's one of the most supportive parents I've ever met. How about giving her a call tonight? Here's the number. Let me know how it goes!" This sets up a positive first exposure.

If Mrs. Malarkey is insecure about her classroom management skills, it's a big deal for her to have her classes videotaped even for self-review. Let her know you appreciate it! If she has never exchanged classroom observation visits with a colleague in all her seven years of teaching, it's a *very* big deal when she opens that door for the first time. She might do it once without your noticing and reinforcing. She might do it twice, or even three times, but if you miss the opportunity to say "Way to go!" early on, she might think "Why bother?" After all, at this point she has moved out of her comfort zone. It's essential that you recognize that shift in direction and let her know you value her participation in the program.

Squint If Necessary

In the book *Dealing with Difficult Teachers* (2002), I discuss the idea of looking for the good parts in everyone—even if you have to squint. Taking this approach can challenge your leadership skills; after all, we're only human. But remember, everyone else is only human, too. Even the most negative forces aren't all negative, all the time.

In discussing Strategy 3, *Determine Who Matters Most*, I mentioned that the backbones could be described with the same adjectives as the superstars if only we added "for the most part" or "most of the time." Well, we can say something similar about the negative forces: "To a certain degree," or "some of the time," they display some of the traits of the superstars and backbones. Even the negative forces are caring or productive or creative, to a certain degree. Some of the time they try hard, follow directions, and put students first.

So let's assume that they want to do what's right or what's best. Let's be sure to recognize their talents, reward their efforts and reinforce the positive. Let's help them change and grow. This is one way to make the most of our most important commodity—our people.

Strategy 9
Fit It All Together

1 | 2 | 3 | 4 | 5 | 6 | 7 | 8 | **9**

Picture the challenge of a Rubik's cube. To solve the puzzle, you have to rotate the pieces until the nine squares on each face show the same color. This may involve working on more than one face at once. Perhaps you have to move two green squares out of place and park them somewhere else while you put a red one where it belongs. Yet even with all the variety of possible moves, there are certain constants. The center square on each side is fixed in place and connected to the center square on the opposite side. No matter what you do, the center squares stay in three sets of opposites. Everything else rotates around them.

By now, it should be clear that this book isn't a straightforward, by-the-numbers instruction manual for operating a machine. The strategies I've outlined here can be put to work in any setting, and no two leaders will employ them in the same way. You may emphasize one strategy in one situation and give more weight to another in a different situation. The process of change is multifaceted and far from linear. As with Rubik's cube, there are certain constants that make it easier to fit all of the pieces together, and I'd like to close by highlighting a few of these tried-and-true approaches.

Make Sure the Change Matters

People don't resist change as such, they resist having change imposed upon them for the sake of change. One reason some experienced educators regard proposed changes with a healthy dose of skepticism is that they have encountered so many new ideas, plans, and programs, each one advertised as better than the one before. Early in their careers, they may have readily jumped on the bandwagon and done the work to make the change, only to find that when the wind shifted or a new leader came to town, all their past efforts no longer mattered.

Never lose sight of the one crucial fact that what really makes a difference in your school is the people, not the programs. Remember that people only have so much time, energy, and effort to give. Before you bring in yet another new concept, you need to make sure it is worth the resources it will consume. Don't move forward without consulting your best people, the ones with the broadest vision. Ask the key questions: What is best for our students? What is best for our school? Will this change meet our needs and help us to grow?

Be Willing to Back Off

The corollary to making sure the change matters is staying alert to the possibility that in some cases, the change you seek is just not a good fit for your school at this time. Pay attention to your instincts in the early stages. Keep an open mind and an open door; let others know that your plans are not carved in stone. As you evaluate how things are going, be willing to discontinue efforts that are not going well in order to achieve the goals that matter most.

Make It about Improvement

Throughout this book, I have spoken about leading change. However, I hope that your efforts really involve leading *improvement*. Change can come easily, all too easily if leadership skills are lacking. Anyone can let an organization take the path of least resistance; anyone can let people drift into inattentive habits of mind and unproductive patterns of behavior. The challenge is to keep an organization and its people moving forward on the path of growth.

When I lead workshops on dealing with difficult teachers and ask participants to describe their characteristics, they often comment that difficult teachers are resistant to change, but when I ask for specific examples, time after time it turns out that these individuals dig in their heels when we ask them to improve their practices, because that almost invariably involves work. As leaders, we need to stay focused on improving our schools, and we need to remember that the only way to improve a school is to lead the people in it to improve.

Follow the 100-Hour Rule

How many times have you attended a workshop or conference presentation where you encountered ideas that really inspired you, or an approach that seemed as if it would really make a difference in your school? Do you remember what happened next?

If you're like most people, you couldn't wait to get back to work so you could start spreading the word about the New Big Idea and take the first steps toward putting it into practice. On your desk you found stacks of papers to grade, or a list of phone calls to return, or a schedule that included two important meetings. You told yourself you would deal with these matters of immediate urgency and *then* get back to the New Big Idea, but if you're like most people, other urgent matters came up, and then the next weekend rolled around and family plans took precedence. Before you knew it, the New Big Idea had slipped from your mind. When you cleaned off your desk at the end of the school year, you found your notes and pamphlets from the workshop, but somehow they didn't rekindle the same feeling of energy and excitement.

As I said, this happens to most of us, more than we'd like. One way to keep it from happening in the future is to follow what I like to call the 100-hour rule. In essence, this rule suggests that if you are energized by that New Big Idea, you have about 100 hours to begin to take action. If you miss that window of opportunity, it is likely you never will follow through.

The time frame of 100 hours is arbitrary, of course. Other rules of thumb suggest that the momentum for action persists for anywhere from five hours to five days. But the point is the same: To keep the New Big Idea from joining all the others that have gone before, you must do something with it right away.

Now, you might remember that under Strategy 2, *Make the First Exposure Great!*, I advised against rushing back from that workshop to tell colleagues all about it. It's true that you'll want to be intentional about bringing the New Big Idea to your school, but beginning to take action doesn't mean starting right down that path toward change. It just means doing something to mark the path so you don't get permanently sidetracked. For example, if you attend a workshop on project-based learning in April and it sounds like a good fit for your school, you might make a note on your draft agenda for the end-of-year leadership team meeting: "Distribute materials on project-based learning." Mark your calendar for the week before with a reminder to prepare the packets.

Other ideas for keeping the New Big Idea on your radar screen might be as simple as bookmarking the workshop leader's Website on your browser's home page, or signing up for a weekly email bulletin from the sponsoring organization. If you attend the conference as part of a group from your school or district, beginning to take action might mean that before you head home, you set a lunch date to pull everyone back together to discuss the concepts.

The 100-hour rule doesn't necessarily mean that you never put anything on the back burner; you have to do this at times. It just means that when you do put the New Big Idea on the back burner, you keep it simmering—and you set the timer on the stove so the New Big Idea doesn't boil away to nothing while your attention is elsewhere. Taking action while you're still energized by that first positive exposure may help you remember to do something about it at the opportune time.

Set the Pace

When we reflect on change efforts that have fallen short of their goals, one complaint we often hear is that someone tried to change things too fast. This may or may not be true. Keep in mind that "too fast" is a relative judgment. For those who really don't want to change, even a snail's pace is too fast. Many times, when people say "Go slow," what they really mean is "No go!" So how can you know how to pace your efforts to implement change?

There is no fixed rule. One useful indicator is whether all of the key players are on board. As described under Strategy 7, *Look Past Buy-in to Action,* you can track this with a graphic web that maps the progress of buy-in. The superstars are normally open to change; if they're holding back, it may mean that the concept is inappropriate for your setting or that your plans need more work. Talk with them, and listen closely to what they say. If they really are on board, give them the time they need to bring along as many others as possible. Check back with them about the concerns others may raise. By allowing the spread of buy-in to guide the pace of change, you can significantly reduce the risk of taking what one disgruntled teacher dubbed the "Ready, Fire, Aim" approach.

Choose the Time

As we saw when discussing Strategy 1, *Identify the Change,* even a straightforward procedural change can seem like a big deal. Even small changes can seem disruptive if they just keep coming, one after another. If you reroute the flow of hallway traffic one week, tweak the lunch schedule the next week, and change the fire drill plan the week after that, everyone starts to feel unsettled. It's often easier and more effective over time to make several changes all at once, providing support as people become accustomed to the new routine. As we've said, the best time to make such changes is often the beginning of the school year.

In my experience, most people are on their best behavior at the start of school. The students are quieter and more responsive; teachers have fresh plan books; even the attendance records and gradebooks are a clean slate. Before the culture settles back into familiar patterns, you have a window of opportunity to make procedural and structural changes that can establish new and better patterns. The first faculty meeting is the best time to set fresh expectations and introduce new dynamics, especially if you've rearranged the furniture in the meeting room over the summer.

This window of opportunity is an annual event: School starts fresh every year. However, two other events offer equally promising openings for introducing change, although these occur less often. The first occurs when a school moves into a new facility. The new setting alters so many aspects of the daily routine that it becomes easier to realign the foundation for better performance in every area. This would be an excellent time to implement changes aimed at improving the culture of the school.

The second opportunity arises when a new leader comes to the school or district. Again, everybody is on their best behavior. They know that the new era of leadership will bring change; that's a given. They expect a fresh approach, different expectations, and new dynamics. If you're the new leader, don't disappoint them! Make the new direction clear from the start.

Let me give a relatively trivial example of what this means. Say that for years, staff members at Riverdale High have answered incoming calls by simply stating their name in a friendly tone of voice: "Mrs. Jefferson" or "Mr. Lincoln." A new principal who would rather have a different greeting, "Good morning, Riverdale High School Library" or "Good afternoon, Riverdale High School Guidance Office," would do well to make this known on the very first day. The same change introduced a month later might be perceived as criticism or correction.

Again, this is a very trivial example, at the level of procedural change, but the same principle applies to structural and cultural changes. A new principal who intends to change the nature and timing of in-house professional development (a structural change) as a means of improving the way the school approaches teaching and learning (a cultural change) would do well to make this crystal clear during the very first faculty meeting.

Frame It as Their Idea

Teachers and leaders in any setting face the same challenge: motivating people to do what we want or need them to do. Clearly, some people are better at this than others; the superstars in our schools can get their students to do almost anything. One key tactic is to make any change seem like their idea, not your idea. If they view it as their idea, they almost always like it. However, if they see it as your idea, it may not go over so well!

Under Strategy 4, *Find the Entry Points*, I described how a principal could introduce the idea of teachers videotaping their performance for self-directed development by commenting that several faculty members had inquired about it and that video crews had been lined up, ready to meet this need. Under Strategy 6, *Harness the Power of Emotion*, we saw how Mrs. Proactive continued this theme while indirectly encouraging wider participation, using phrases like "so many of you say how valuable you have found this practice" and "several of you had expressed concern about how quickly you have been going through DVDs." Likewise, having teachers volunteer positive feedback about their Dial It Up phone calls makes a much better impression than insisting from behind the podium that more people should get on board with this practice.

Take the Shotgun Approach

Years ago, cars didn't even have seatbelts. Even after they were introduced, the safety devices often went unused. Then several things happened: Seatbelts became standard equipment; television ads, billboards, and newspaper articles touting the use and safety of seatbelts proliferated; states passed laws mandating their use; highway signs at interstate on-ramps reminded drivers to "buckle up for safety," and safety education programs targeted elementary school students. Now, most people use seatbelts as a matter of course, saying they feel naked without them. Drivers remind their passengers to buckle up; passengers remind the driver. Children insist that their parents wear seatbelts, and they'll holler if the car starts to move before their own are secured. It's hard to say which of these developments tipped the balance, but the new idea has become normal.

School leaders embarking on change should take a similarly multipronged approach. Combine all of the strategies described here, mixing and matching to adjust to your particular situation. The broader and more diverse your campaign, the more difficult it will be to resist and the sooner the new will seem normal.

Make Your Toolbox Part of the Furniture

During my years as a principal, I identified a number of practices that I believe constitute essential tools of the trade. I've written about them in greater detail in other books, and you may have noticed a number of them here:

- the weekly staff memo I call the *Friday Focus*
- the habit of dropping in to observe classes, briefly but so frequently that the students and teacher hardly notice
- the purposeful arrangement of the room where staff meetings take place
- the notes of appreciation I send to staff members for contributions to the school climate, large and small
- the phone calls to inform parents when their children do the right thing, not just when they do the wrong thing

As school leaders, we can't put off using these tools until the moment when we need them to implement change. We have to use them so often that everyone becomes accustomed to them as part of the routine. Otherwise, they become part of the change, and that makes the whole enterprise more difficult.

Consider Strategy 8, *Reinforce Changed Behavior*. This is much more effective if taking the positive approach happens all the time. If I send out the *Friday Focus* memo about teachers getting out from behind their desks to interact with students, any unannounced classroom visits I make during the next several days will look more like a "Gotcha!" than a "Way to go!" unless I've made dropping in a longstanding habit.

Or consider Strategy 5, *Reduce the Resistence* I suggested that rearranging the seating in the room where faculty meetings are held would help break up a cluster of negative staff members, but if you do this for the first time before a meeting in which you introduce a major change, you will throw everyone into confusion. Instead, start well ahead of time to improve the dynamics of staff meetings in your school. Then any topic you introduce is more likely to be well received.

Likewise, it's important to build good relationships before you need them. I've heard people suggest starting off a difficult conference with parents by making two positive statements about their child. In my experience, this is more likely to be perceived as a ploy to get the parents on your side than as honest praise. It's much more effective to make positive communication with parents a part of your everyday practices.

Seek the Support of Support Staff

Among the relationships that we should build ahead of time and keep in good working order are those with support staff. Whether or not they are directly involved in implementing a change, support staff can play a critical role in promoting acceptance for an idea. This may be especially true with the world outside of school. When major change is on the horizon, the rumor mill starts to churn. If your good-natured custodian plays cards with a group of local citizens, the conversation may turn to the New Big Idea that you're just about to put into practice. It sure is helpful if the custodian can comment, "Yeah, they've been planning that for quite a while. It looks as if they're really taking the time to do it right. From what I've seen, it's going to be great for the kids."

Manage the Rumor Mill

When change is afoot, effective leaders keep it out in the open through regular communication with everyone involved, both inside and outside the organization. Otherwise, the teachers' lounge, the secretarial pool, and the bus barn can become the breeding ground for rumors—and rumors don't creep; they fly!

> "I saw people boxing up all the history books in the library—I wonder if they've decided to get rid of them because students do all their research on the Internet these days?"
>
> "I heard they're taking all the books out of the library!"
> "I saw the maintenance staff going in there with cleaning supplies, three days in a row."
>
> "Someone told me there's a major mildew problem, and it will take thousands of dollars to fix!"

In fact, the maintenance staff routinely cleans one section of shelves each summer.

Here's where the weekly *Friday Focus* bulletin comes in handy. You can send it to everyone in the community who has a vested interest in your school—not just the teachers and administrators, but everyone on the support staff. To widen its impact, you could send a copy to the district superintendent and to other principals in the area as well.

Make It Happen—Together

Even the most effective leader would have difficulty imposing change from above. The only way to really move your school forward is to work together, as a team. As you make your plans and do your best to bring everybody on board, I hope you'll put these nine strategies to good use. I wish you well on your journey to school improvement and growth!

We also recommend:

Motivating and Inspiring Teachers:
The Educational Leader's Guide for Building
Staff Morale, 2nd Edition
Todd Whitaker, Beth Whitaker, and Dale Lumpa

"Thank you, thank you, thank you. Every one of Todd Whitaker's books has changed the perception and manner in which I guide my school. They are truly inspiring."
> Donald Merkel, Assistant Principal
> Garland High School, TX

Like the best-selling first edition, this book is filled with strategies to motivate and stimulate your staff. It includes simple suggestions which you can integrate into your current daily routine. It shows you how to:
- Insert key phrases and specific actions into your day-today conversations, staff meetings, and written memos to encourage peak effectiveness
- Cultivate and retain loyal and motivated staff members
- Motivate yourself each and every day

The second edition includes four new chapters for improving and sustaining morale:
- Teacher Leaders—Build morale with the support of key staff members
- Sharpening Your Focus—Learn how to make your staff memo even better
- Showing Off Your School—Let everyone know about your school's success
- Feeling Better through Fitness and Wellness—Help teachers take care of themselves

2010, 272 pp. paperback 1-5966-7103-4 $39.95 plus shipping and handling

What Great Teachers Do *Differently*:
14 Things That Matter Most
Todd Whitaker

"This book is easy to read and provides essential information. I've ordered copies for every one of my teachers."

> Anne Ferrell, Principal
> Autrey Hill Middle School
> Alpharetta, Georgia

This #1 best selling book has been widely adopted in study groups and professional development programs across the country. It describes the beliefs, behaviors, attitudes, and interactions that form the fabric of life in our best classrooms and schools. It focuses on the specific things that great teachers do...that others do not.

It answers these essential questions —

- Is it high expectations for students that matter?
- How do great teachers respond when students misbehave?
- Do great teachers filter differently than their peers?
- How do the best teachers approach standardized testing?
- How can your teachers gain the same advantages?

2004, 144 pp. paperback 1-930556-69-1 $29.95 plus shipping and handling

What Great Principals Do *Differently*:
15 Things That Matter Most
Todd Whitaker

"...filled with common sense suggestions for making our jobs more rewarding."

> Jim Collins, Director
> Professional Development
> School Administrators Assoc.
> New York State

What are the specific qualities and practices of great principals that elevate them above the rest? Blending school-centered studies and experiences working with hundreds of administrators, the author reveals the 15 things that the most successful principals do and that other principals do not.

Topics include—

- It's People, Not Programs
- Who is the Variable?
- The Principal Is the Filter
- Teach the Teachers
- Base Every Decision on Your Best Teachers
- Make It Cool to Care

2002, 130 pp. paperback 1-930556-47-0 $29.95 plus shipping and handling

Seven Simple Secrets:
What the BEST Teachers Know and Do!
Annette Breaux and Todd Whitaker

"There is no one I can recommend more highly than Annette Breaux."

Harry K. Wong, author
The First Days of School

This book reveals—

- The Secret of Classroom Management
- The Secret of Instruction
- The Secret of Attitude
- The Secret of Professionalism
- The Secret of Effective Discipline
- The Secret of Motivation and Inspiration

Implementing these secrets will change your life, both in and out of the classroom. But most importantly, implementing these secrets will enhance the lives of every student you teach.

2006, 160 pp. paperback 1-59667-021-5 $29.95 plus shipping and handling

Todd Whitaker on Audio CD

What Great Teachers Do *Differently* Audio CD

World-renowned author and speaker Todd Whitaker describes the beliefs, behaviors, and attitudes of our best teachers. Based on a live recording of a Todd Whitaker presentation, the tracks include—

- The Standard of Greatness
- Random versus Plandom
- Ten Days Out of Ten
- Building Trust
- Making It Cool to Care
- Great Teachers Make the Difference

11 tracks on two CDs totaling 2 hours

2009, 978-1-59667-115-1 $49.95 plus shipping and handling

What Great Principals Do *Differently* Audio CD

In this live recording of a Todd Whitaker presentation, the world-renowned author speaks directly to listeners about the specific things that great principals do...that others do not. The tracks include—

- Leadership Styles
- It's People, Not Programs
- Three Kinds of Teachers
- Repair and Change
- You are the Filter
- Raise the Praise, Minimize the Criticize

6 tracks on two CDs totaling 2 hours

2009, 978-1-59667-117-1 $49.95 plus shipping and handling

Free Preview Clips at www.eyeoneducation.com

Bring Todd Whitaker to Your School!
Todd Whitaker...on DVD!

"It is amazing how much substance is packed into this presentation… our attention never wanders. This DVD holds up a mirror so we can look at ourselves and our classroom practices through a new set of eyes."

Rick Wormeli
Best-selling Author
and Consultant

What Great Teachers Do *Differently* DVD
This $499 package includes—

- 11 programs totaling over two hours
- Facilitator's Guide
- Also included is a copy of the best-selling book **What Great Teachers Do *Differently*: 14 Things That Matter Most**

2007, 1-59667-053-3 $499 plus $13 for shipping and handling.

What Great Principals Do *Differently* DVD
This $499 package includes—

- 6 programs on one DVD totaling over two hours
- Facilitator's Guide
- Also included is a copy of the best-selling book **What Great Principals Do *Differently*: 15 Things That Matter Most**

2007, 1-59667-052-5 $499 plus $13 for shipping and handling.

Use these DVDs in teacher workshops, study groups, or with school improvement teams.

Free Preview Clips at www.eyeoneducation.com

Great Quotes for Great Educators
Todd Whitaker and Dale Lumpa

Over 600 insightful, witty nuggets to motivate and inspire you...
...and everyone else at your school.

Teachers—display these quotes in your classrooms!

Administrators—insert them into your faculty memos and share them at staff meetings!

Why is this book unique?
- includes over 100 original quotes from internationally acclaimed speaker and educator Todd Whitaker
- features real quotes from real students, which echo wit and wisdom for educators
- each quote has a direct connection to your life as an educator

Examples of quotes in this book...

"Great teachers have high expectations for their students, but higher expectations for themselves."
Todd Whitaker

"We can never control a classroom until we control ourselves."
Todd Whitaker

2004, 208 pp. paperback 1-903556-82-9 $29.95 plus shipping and handling

50 WAYS TO IMPROVE STUDENT BEHAVIOR:
Simple Solutions to Complex Challenges
Annette Breaux and Todd Whitaker

"This book is a great resource for teachers, not to be read once and put away, but to be used as a desk reference for a student-centered classroom."

Eve Ford
Director of Student Success Initiatives,
Hallsville Independent School District,
Hallsville, TX

50 Ways to Improve Student Behavior is a must-read reference for teachers, both new and experienced. In a lively and engaging style, Annette Breaux and Todd Whitaker share 50 simple, straightforward techniques for improving student behavior and increasing student cooperation, participation, and achievement. Each practical, well-defined strategy can be applied in classrooms of all grade-levels and subjects.

Strategies include:
- How to nip potential problems in the bud
- Learning what to overlook
- Establishing classroom rules and procedures
- Teaching in small bites (It makes students hungrier!)

As student behavior improves, so too will the quality of learning in your classroom. With this book, you can begin to introduce a host of new techniques into your teaching practice today!

2010, 144 pp. paperback 159667-125-6 $29.95 plus shipping and handling

Teaching Matters:
Motivating & Inspiring Yourself
Todd and Beth Whitaker

"This book makes you want to be the best teacher you can be."
Nancy Fahnstock
Godby High School
Tallahassee, Florida

Celebrate the teaching life! This book helps teachers:

- rekindle the excitement of the first day of school all year long
- approach every day in a "Thank God it is Monday" frame of mind
- not let negative people ruin your day
- fall in love with teaching all over again

Brief Contents

- Why You're Worth it
- Unexpected Happiness
- Could I Have a Refill Please? (Opportunities for Renewal)
- Celebrating Yourself
- Raise the Praise–Minimize the Criticize
- Making School Work for You

2002, 150 pp. paperback 1-930556-35-7 $24.95 plus shipping and handling